O V E 4 ★ X &

The Shape of Engagement

O V E 4 ★ X &

The Art of Creating Enduring Connections
with Your Customers, Employees
and Communities

Scott Gould

First edition published September 2017

ISBN 978-1976095153

OVE4★X&

The Shape
of Engagement

OVE4★X&

To my favourite, who is the only one that
I've engaged with a diamond shape,

there is no other relationship
I'd rather make the most of,

and no other person
who has enabled
me so much.

♥

Contents

Preface

It began with a problem.

When consulting with my clients – from small NGOs, startups, the public sector, and through to Fortune Global 500s – I kept hearing the same complaint from people on the front line of engagement over and over again. They were trying as hard as they could to increase engagement, using tactics that seemed to work one day and then didn't the next, but they had a distinct lack of a strategic framework to guide them, and to help them get to a place of sustainable, consistent engagement.

I, on the other hand, had developed numerous frameworks and concepts for describing how engagement works and could be harnessed, through 18 years of experience in working with people, from running conferences and concerts to broadcasting and television, from aviation to education and to government, and from building online communities to being a church minister.

I had managed to get my frameworks out to a certain degree through client work, seminars, and blogging, but I wanted to do more. At the same time, requests and recommendations for a book that brought my ideas together started coming in, but I wanted to delay this for as long as possible owing to the stacks of research, books, and fascinating people that I waned to draw on to write a full work on the subject. However, to create a short, punchy work that contained the core frameworks in one collection: now that was something I could certainly do in the meantime, and has been my project over the summer of 2017.

Thus, you hold in your hands the result: seven key frameworks for engagement developed over my 18 years in the space.

Being the short book that it is, I regret that this book is without footnotes that would add evidence to my ideas, without case studies that would add far more life to the frameworks, and without discussion of and development on the work of others. Should I have the opportunity to extend on this initial offering and write the fuller work that I have described above, I will certainly address these shortcomings.

Additionally, the litany of people I need to thank for encouraging me and providing suggestions and feedback along the way – which surely numbers into the hundreds – is far more than I can fit into this small volume, and so I also hope I will have the chance to rightfully thank them by name too.

Fortunately, the lack of formally referencing the work of other authors is not too problematic for this short treatment on the subject. The ideas contained within here are the product of my own painstaking work over eight years, during which time I've thought *constantly* about this subject and taken each framework through its paces and numerous redesigns.

However. There are a handful of authors who simply *must* be recognised upfront. These thinkers are the giants upon whose shoulders I have stood, whose ideas provoked and inspired me, and without whom this book would sincerely not be possible.

Thus, let me break the traditional order of books, and ask you to consider this upfront as the bibliography, further reading, and credits, but where it deserves to be: before anything of mine.

First and foremost:

Joe Pine & **James Gilmore** to whom I pay my utmost thanks, gratitude and respect. It was Joe's TED Talk – the first that I ever watched, back in 2008 – that introduced me to their ideas, but more so, opened my eyes to the power of frameworks to expound and understand things. In particular, any use of the word *experience* within this book, especially in Shape 3, the *3-E Maturity Model*, directly relates to their terminology as expounded in their seminal works, *The Experience Economy* and *Authenticity*.

Furthermore, I'm grateful to Joe for his personal support and encouragement over the years. Anyone familiar with Joe and Jim's work will see their thinking runs through mine like blood through veins. It is, therefore, most fitting that Joe graciously offered to write the foreword, for which I am doubly grateful.

The rest are alphabetical:

Ken Blanchard, creator of the *One Minute Manager Series*. My thinking around meaning, purpose and worthwhile work, especially in Shapes 1, 3 and 4, is inspired by his example in *Gung Ho*, which I consider to be the best engagement book on the planet.

Bruce Bolger, co-author of *Enterprise Engagement: The Roadmap*, who was pioneering the field of engagement before most of us were even using the word. He created the concept of enterprise engagement as referenced in Shape 4.

Robert Cialdini, whose succinct book *Influence: Science and Practice* was the textbook from which I lectured at a post-graduate leadership school. After four years of lecturing on the book, his six principles of influence have undoubtedly (and suitably) influenced my work. The granularity of Shapes 5 and 6, and the concept of internal motivators, is particularly influenced by him.

Robin Dickinson, a dear friend who encouraged the early blog posts in 2009 that have led to this book. His life lessons, summarised in his book, *The Fortune 8*, has become part of my life and shaped the way I think. Shape 2 is in the vein of the type of granular conversations we would have, as is the point that engagement is not the end goal, the bigger intention is.

Sam Ford, co-author of *Spreadable Media* along with Henry Jenkins and Joshua Green, who personally encouraged me in the early days of my thinking that I was onto something with the idea of Scattering, Gathering, and Mattering. His work affected Shape 3.

Seth Godin, whose under appreciated book, *Unleashing the Ideavirus* was an early inspiration for my Scatter, Gather, Matter idea. It is a cliché to reference Seth these days, such is his popularity and quotability, but my book would certainly not exist now without his, and thus it rightfully appears here. Shape 1 is inspired by thoughts that originated from reading his work.

Chip & Dan Heath, who through their book *Switch*, taught me the power of using metaphors to make an idea memorable, and the division of reason, emotion, and environment. Shape 5's classification of emotion, mental, action, etc, is developed from their division.

Mark Knapp, creator of Knapp's Relationship Model as framed in his book *Social Intercourse*. I came across his framework after finalising my own relationship model (half of which appears in this book, under Shape 6), which served to corroborate my findings.

Patrick Lencioni, who with *The Five Dysfunctions of a Team*, showed me how to use shapes as frameworks, which has become the very concept of this book. His model was an inspiration for how my presentation of Shapes 2, 3 and 5, and in my understanding of employee engagement, reflected in Shape 4.

Charlene Li & **Josh Bernoff,** who created the participation ladder in *Groundswell* that inspired me to work on my own version in 2009. That evolved considerably to appear here as Shape 6.

Simon Sinek, creator of the Golden Circle and author of *Start With Why*. Along with the millions that have watched his TED Talk, he made the word WHY come alive for me, as well as the other members of Kipling's Six Honest Men. The simplicity of Shape 1, I hope, echoes the simplicity of his Golden Circle.

David Taylor, who wrote the curiously titled *The Naked Leader*. One idea in that book, about connecting with people by finding things in common to talk about, changed my life when I read it some 15 years ago. The S in Shape 5 is inspired by that revelation.

Thank you all.

Scott Gould,
Plymouth, UK

Foreword to
The Shape of Engagement

B. Joseph Pine II

What a beautiful little book you have in your hands (or on your screen)! I love every model in it, for each one will enable you to deepen the experiences you stage as well as the relationships you have with your customers, your employees, the community in which you serve, and – see Shape 4! – yourself.

Scott Gould – whom I consider my friend with the highest ratio of relationship to time physically spent together – has marshalled an impressive set of ideas and frameworks (with this wonderful connective tissue: shape) all centered on the topic of engagement.

And what an important topic it is! When I work with companies on embracing the Experience Economy and want people to understand the distinction between staging experiences and (merely) delivering services, manufacturing goods, or extracting commodities, the crucial term is exactly that: engagement. You must engage your customers in order to stage a true, distinctive experience, an experience that reaches inside of them and creates a memory within them that lasts long after the experience recedes. And, of course, if you want to create an engaging experience for customers, you first must make sure you engage your employees, giving them the wherewithal to perform on your business stage.

Each and every model Scott takes you through deepens the experiences you stage, taking you on a journey as simple as 1, 2, 3. And then 4, 5, 6, and 7! He is a master at creating, forming, and explaining frameworks that will enable (see Shape 3!) you to understand, internalize, and then operationalize them in your business and, not insignificantly, in your life.

And that is something I do not say lightly. I have joked with my partner Jim Gilmore that we should have named our business Frameworks 'R' Us, for that is what we excel at. My purpose in work is to figure out what is going on in the world of business and then develop frameworks that first describe what is happening and then prescribe what businesses can and should do about it.

I now see a kindred spirit in Scott, and am honored to have inspired him to train his discerning eye on engagement.

So do not miss the opportunity to engage with this book, wrestle with its ideas and frameworks, and then use them to make a difference in your business, as well as your life, your community, and the world.

B. Joseph Pine II
Dellwood, Minnesota

Co-founder, *Strategic Horizons LLP*
Author, *The Experience Economy*, *Authenticity*, *Mass Customization*, and *Infinite Possibility: Creating Customer Value on the Digital Frontier*

OVE4＊X＆

Prologue

Love life. Engage in it. Give it all you've got.
Love it with a passion because life truly does give back,
many times over, what you put into it.
— Maya Angelou

Life is engagement.

We're either constantly engaging, or constantly being pulled on to engage: *Engage with your work, engage with your colleagues, engage with your kids. Engage with the customer, engage with the stakeholders, engage with the idea. Engage in the conversation, engage in the process, engage in life.* It's a lot. And it's pretty much all of us at one point or another throughout the course of any given day.

There are those of us who are even required to get others engaged: *Get your students engaged. Get your employees engaged. Get your customer engaged. Get your community engaged. Get your citizens engaged.* And here the story goes two ways.

For some of these people, the work they do to engage others is a journey of joy, unlocking value through enduring connections and shared aspirations, and bringing out the best in people and their organisations as they go.

But for others, the E-word is an uphill struggle, with every attempt they make to engage seemingly falling on deaf ears and folded arms, gaining little to no response.

And the difference between the two is very often the difference between failure and success. We whose work is engagement know this well. We know the impact you can make as an engaged team where people are dedicated and committed, as opposed to one that is distracted, unfocussed, and with a jobsworth mentality. We know the joy of interacting with an engaged customer; one who is a believer, who is a passionate advocate, and bears with us when things go wrong; as opposed to the unengaged, demanding yet undedicated customers who drain energy rather than create it. And we know that it is the engaged community members who roll up their sleeves and make things happen, in contrast to the unengaged masses who want results but don't take any responsibility.

It used to be that engagement didn't matter as much. It was possible to have the fastest machine, the sweetest carrot, the loudest drum, and for that to be enough for you to get the outcome you wanted, whether that was increasing profits, productivity or achieving your chosen purpose.

But those days are far, far behind us.

Today competition is fierce, commoditisation is happening fast, and commitment wanes all too quickly amidst the demands of our time-pressured lives. Organisations that thrived on silos and distance from people are struggling in a world where more than ever before, access is democratised, data is a commodity, on-demand services have disrupted command and control, and the digital revolution that has causes much of this is likely still only warming up.

What does it take to cut through this? Engagement.

Engagement is to deal in those things and to make the most of a relationship. It's to dive down into the depths of a human heart and draw out that value that is born only from an enduring connection, and motivated by those things that are far beyond the grasp of price or convenience. Things like enablement. Things like community, communion and collaboration. Things like purpose, meaning, vision, and mission.

I'm reminded of ad man Bill Bernbach's exhortation to marketers not to be concerned with *changing* humanity, but rather to make their focus *unchanging* humanity, those things that have remained and will remain the same about us: our hopes, fears, desire for connection, need for affirmation, and thirst of meaning.

This is the stuff of enduring connection, far from the commoditised, skin deep and cheap, fleeting malaise of a brief, ephemeral connection: where what engages comes and goes, at best becoming an memory of something that happened once, but more likely, being utterly forgotten.

Ephemeral Connection vs. Enduring Connection

Unengaged	Engaged
Uncommitted	Committed
Unloyal	Loyal
Low retention	High retention
High churn	Low churn
Low motivation	High motivation

Numerous studies show time and time again that organisations where employees are engaged and customers are engaged are more productive and more profitable. Some studies put an engaged customer as being 300% more valuable per year than an unengaged customer, while others say an engaged workforce will drive an increase of 19.2% in operating income.

(Statistics and sources at shapeofengagementbook.com.)

Whatever the numbers, the result is that when engaged, employees and customers are both more loyal, more committed, and more invested, and the net result is that it creates value for all, including the company and its shareholders, to the tune of an average 29.9% increase in stock price (as per the Engaged Company Stock Index, TheEEA.org.)

Do you want to be one of those organisations? Sure you do. But so do your competitors. And with the idea of enterprise engagement spreading, they are doing what they can to engage first and to engage the most. Don't forget inertia either, which wants to keep your community in the old and away from the new.

Yet, in the midst of this seemingly frenetic world of change, there is an opportunity. People still, as they always have done, and always will do, are crying out for purpose, meaning and enablement. And what most are not doing is finding out how to tap into that, because few know how to do it.

For the longest time the work of engagement has been somewhat of a mystery, with most finding their way through it by trying hit-and-miss tactics in the hope that, in the end, they'll strike lucky with success. Why is that? Why have we lacked strategy for such noble work at this?

From what I've seen, I believe it is because many people who are engaging as individuals have found their way into careers of service more often than those of business. They go into health care, social work, the voluntary sector, local government, relief work, education, community work, religious service, and the like. Accordingly, this ability to engage is a skill set that has been sorely missed in enterprise in general.

Additionally, these people have then all been too busy doing the work of engagement and serving others, so that they've had less time to tell the rest of us how to do it, as well as finding themselves in careers that traditionally author business literature less frequently. I can certainly attest for myself that what I've learned about engagement came first from my time as a church pastor, secondly as a lover of people in general, and only then from my work in business. Perhaps that's because of the career path I took, but I think there's more to it than that.

There is also another issue. Engagement has quickly become a technical term: we talk about customer engagement, employee engagement, and community engagement, but few seem to agree on what the word engagement actually means when it relates to our work. It doesn't help that the word is both an adjective and a verb; something can be engaging or engaging! Thus, we might need to clear that up first.

Defining engagement

Here I offer my definition of engagement, which I do not view or intend to be as an improvement on other's renderings, nor as an attempt to rewrite the dictionary (!), but as an exercise in clarity and simplicity. I offer it as a definition that can apply to any use of the word *engage*, or its derivatives, such as *engagement*, *engaged*, or *engaging*. So that includes say a film being engaging, through to a company being engaging, and to one being engaged to be married!

So in it's most essential form, here is my definition.

The definition of engagement:
Engagement is the process of making the most of a relationship

When we say that we are engaging with someone or something it is to say we endeavour to make the most of that relationship.

This is critically important in the business of any organisation today. Where most organisations are forced to compete on price or salary, it is those organisations that are able to engage their customers, employees and communities on the level of purpose, meaning, mission, community and enablement, that are the organisations securing the top talent, making the most difference, and creating the most value.

It then follows that to make the most of a relationship we need to *give our most to the relationship*. This too is very important, and whilst perhaps it will be assumed by readers of this book, we should clarify it now: engagement is work. Now of course, anything worth doing is work, but engagement will be work on top of existing work, at least at first. The benefit of engagement is that as you give the most *to* the relationship you also get the most *from* the relationship because both parties are making the most *of* the relationship, and that is something quite exponential indeed.

I should probably say that again, for it's easy to miss it:

We get the most from the relationships that we give the most to.

That goes for our friendships, our children, our work colleagues, our team members, our community members, our clients, and without a doubt, our customers. Engaging relationships of that ilk without our organisations are the dynamic that launch era-defining products, give birth to bold new ideas, and nurture world changers.

There's also another reason why I've settled on this definition (for now). Running parallel to engagement is another process, one that we shan't touch on in this book, but bears mention at least. It is the misuse of engagement, the process of similar dynamics which, rather than fostering healthy engagement, foster manipulation and control. I call this *Dark Engagement*, or *Enslavement*, and the definition of it, in contrast to definition of engagement above, is to *take* the most from a relationship. I hope to write about it one day, indeed, putting it in here is a little accountability nudge to myself, but for now I'll just leave it there.

Engagement is relationship

You will have no doubt noticed by now that I'm heavily blurring the lines between professional and personal relationship, and weaving comparisons of customers, employees, community members, and then kinship and friendship into the same thought.

This is intentional.

It isn't that I view relationships as a metaphor. My premise is that the way we engage with products, brands, and ideas, is the same way that we engage with any human relationship. In my mind, the way we build a relationship with our phone follows the same process for how we build a relationship with a person.

My definition of engagement is 'making the most of a relationship', and that's exactly what we have with the entities that we engage with. The adverts that we don't even notice are strangers to us. But those that we begin to engage with are those we begin to relate to and have a relationship with. It is the same for work, for our communities, for the people we interact with throughout each day, and for the ideas and messages that come into our purview.

I find this makes engagement all the more easy to understand. We can simplify the act of 'trying to understand the buyers mind' when we think about a brand, because we can think about how we relate to a person. Employee and community engagement likewise become simpler because we ask ourselves the golden rule: how would *we* want to be engaged?

Who this book is for

This book is for the executives, managers, strategists and practitioners who work on the frontline of engagement. It'll help you with your broad organisational strategy, and it'll help you with how you write that next email to your team.

If you're holding this book then it's likely that you're one of those people, and further more, that you're one of those people who knows the joy of engaging, who sees value in people at every turn, regardless of what their relationship to the organisation is, but who has also been frustrated by the rarity of strategic frameworks for sustainable, successful engagement.

This book is for you. This book aims to demystify what engagement is, how it works, and how you can inspire other people to engage with you.

We're going to achieve this by walking through a sequence of seven shapes. Each one is a framework that explains a facet of engagement through a simple and memorable shape that you can use again and again, both tactically on the frontline, and strategically in the board room.

And what if you're *not* one of those people? Either you've made a big mistake, or you're about to embark on one thrill ride of a journey. I believe it's the second. So buckle up. You're about to discover something that those of us whose work is people know is the secret to any success.

And why shapes?

Well, to clarify upfront, this book is not trying to break the Da Vinci code! The reason is actually one of engagement. Shapes and symbols are profoundly memorable, and they are everywhere. So as a way of encouraging people to engage with a series of frameworks and concepts (which can often be a bit obtuse and abstract), grounding them in common shapes that you see everyday serves as an excellent memory and recall device.

Making the most of this book

To help you get the most value from this book, all the models are available as a free download online. The package includes:

- The frameworks in a slide deck for presentations
- An executive summary of the book for your team
- A list of key engagement statistics and sources
- High-resolution colour images of the shapes
- Diagnostic forms to audit your engagement
- Expanded editions of the frameworks

Download for free at shapeofengagementbook.com.

OVE4⭑X&

O

The Circle of Engagement

How does engagement happen?

Imagine with me for a moment if you will.

Once upon a time a farmer sowed some seeds into a field. The farmer wanted to feed both his family and the village. So he took his bag of seed and began scattering it in his field. Some seed fell by the rocks, some was eaten by the birds, and some couldn't stand the elements. But that didn't matter, because some fell on good soil, and it grew roots, matured and eventually produced a large harvest. When the crop was ready, the farmer took his sickle and began reaping the harvest, gathering into binds as he went. After the harvest had been gathered, it was prepared and taken to the market. There the villagers could take it to make meals for their families, just like the farmer did for his own family too. The farmer has created something that mattered to people. And finally, when everyone was fed, there was seed left over from the harvest to start the process again…

Or consider a conversation: once upon a time Fred wanted to talk about The Beatles. But Sally wasn't really interested. However when Fred happened to change the conversation to literature, Sally lit up, and they had a really engrossing, participatory conversation. Little surprise, then, that the next time they got together, Fred didn't even think about The Beatles: they picked up where they left off talking about literature, but this time about they focussed on *The Lord of The Rings*, as Sally was currently reading it. And so the process continued...

Or finally, imagine a new website that wanted to have pictures of college students, but the students wanted it to be more than photos, they wanted to include updates. So the website allowed people to make updates. But then the students had friends who weren't students who wanted to use the website. So they let those people have profiles and make updates too. And each time someone new signed up, they could invite *their* friends to the platform. And on the process went...

I'm sure you've got the idea here. You'll likely recognise the biblical origins of the first example, no doubt see yourself in the second example at times (whether you're a LOTR fan or not!), and I don't need to tell you that Facebook is the third example. These examples describe the *Circle of Engagement* and the three inexorable, irreducible, irrefutable processes that comprise it.

O

The Circle of an Engagement is just that – a circle, or the letter O – and just like a circle, engagement is an infinite loop. The circular motion is made of the three processes: Scatter, Gather and Matter.

As we are about to see, Scatter is the beginning of engagement, the outbound part where someone or something puts out a message. Gather is about how people then respond to that message. Finally, Matter is about taking what has from gathering, and turning that into a lasting resource.

The Matter process then feeds back into the Scatter process, the same way that the seed is in the fruit in the farming analogy above.

These three processes, Scatter, Gather, and Matter will be a constant thread throughout each framework because they are how all engagement happens, whether it is with communities or customers, whether it's personal or professional, and even down to the way you're interacting with this book right now.

The Circle of Engagement

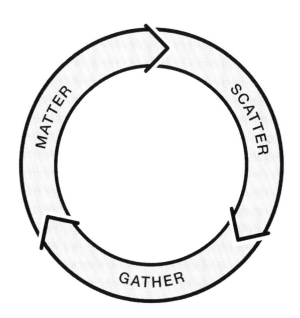

Scatter

All engagement begins with a message. It is the seed to the farmer, the first line in the conversation, and the idea of the university student. Call it what you will – an offering, an invitation, an advertisement, a look in the eyes, a request, an outstretched hand, a speech, or a brand – but it always begins with this. You can't get away from it. We understand this from stimulus-response theory: everything begins with a stimulus. Indeed, it's logical, as there must be a start to a relationship with any entity, the first role of the dice, as it were; and for engagement, it is the message.

And a message is a thing that is scattered. That's the process. A message not scattered is a message not seen. It remains a thought, like product in storage, or a request not made. As we'll see in a moment, we need to embrace scattering to make our message spread. But we're getting ahead of ourselves. Let's restate again, as we did above, what engagement begins with:

The first thing of engagement is a *message*

A message can be almost anything you can think of. We gave some examples above. It could also be an apology, a demand, an enticement, or perhaps a piece of information. It could be a picture, words, colours, a gesture, or any other symbol or sign. It can come in the form of a book, a film, a conversation, a leaflet, a sign, or maybe an SMS. It's the STOP sign in the road, the instructions on your microwave, and the impassioned plea of a world leader. Most of the products we use are messages themselves, emblazoned with brand symbols that all can see: like that nod from our polo shirt or maybe the lit up logo on the back of our laptop. All of these are messages, and we are constantly being bombarded by them, all day, everyday; each and every one of them an attempt to engage us. It's everywhere in the world of work, too. Think of your request to your employees, your marketing to your customers, your mission to your community, and how you communicate these. Everything you create that seeks to touch someone and to elicit even the smallest amount of action, from the simplest of emails, to the grandest of campaigns, is a message.

Think of the message as an invitation to engage. It's not just information. It's not just entertainment. It's an invitation.

It's between *initiator* and *receiver*

The entity (such as a person, brand, idea, product, organisation) that begins the engagement is the *initiator*. They aren't the engager, because actually, both parties will be engaging. But they did initiate the engagement.

On the other side, we have the receiver. A message is either sent, or not sent, and either received or not. But if and when one receives it, they are by definition a *receiver*. So we have the initiator, the sender of the message, and the receiver, who is the recipient.

Receiving the message is the prerequisite for someone to begin the journey of engagement with the one who wishes to engage them. A message can be scattered, but if it is not acknowledged as being received – which is to say it goes unseen, like email into the spam folder – then engagement has not begun.

However! The receiver will not stay as a receiver. As they go through each process, they'll have a different relationships with the initiator. Accordingly, their title will change. But for now, they begin as a receiver.

The message should be *scattered!*

The title of this process underlines the way a message is put out: it is *scattered*, and to state the obvious, scattered does not mean precise, it means chance! Before you overreact to that statement, let's first consider the nature of messages. It is the case in life that we are messaging in far greater volume than we are receiving, and we can't help it. It's a logical necessity: just as light cannot help but shine, a message cannot help but scatter itself everywhere it is seen. To exist is to emanate a message: at the very least, that message states that you exist! (Whether others receive that message is of course another thing, and one we'll examine shortly.)

In our communication, marketing, promotion, speaking, advertising, requests and PR, we are also constantly messaging. A public speaker will speak for 40 minutes but it might be only one phrase that a particular audience member connects with. However because there are hundreds of people in the audience, by messaging more there are multiple chances and hooks for individuals to engage with.

Therefore rather than avoiding the inevitable, those who engage will embrace the scattering nature of the message, and understand that scattering accepts the role of chance. We never fully know who is going to engage with us in return, and seeing as we'll always be scattering more than we're receiving anyway, let's embrace it and scatter broadly to widen the opportunity for people to respond. This understanding liberates us: there is nothing wrong with a person not responding to our message, because it will always be the case that some respond and others don't: that's the nature of seed, the nature of the ground, and the nature of the elements. Perhaps your product isn't what they need right now. Perhaps a certain point in your speech didn't hit home for them. Perhaps there's something going on their life. Perhaps your company isn't the right fit for the employee you're trying to engage: but don't worry, it will be the right fit for someone else. On the other hand, this also means that those we haven't considered will often be the ones who *do* respond. All of us have had times where we thought a business deal or arrangement would come from one source, but the person we expected to respond didn't, and instead someone we didn't expect was the one who *did* respond to the opportunity. Thus open handed scattering inclines us to this kind of serendipity.

- What messages have you received today? Consider things like visual cues, reading, signage, branding, emails and face to face communication.
- What messages have you and/or your organisation scattered today? How are you inviting or not inviting people to engage with you?
- If your organisation was a person, what type of impression would your customers, employees or communities have of it?

Gather

When the seed that the farmer has scattered has become a harvest, then the crop will be gathered, and when someone connects with a point in a conversation, they reply. In the same way, when someone responds to a message they are gathering around that message.

The moment that we respond, the moment in which we gather, could be when we accept an apology, walk into a store as a result of an advert, shake someone's hand in return, download an app, reply to an email thread, pick up a book off the shelf, ask someone what brand they are using, respond in a conversation, or attend an event. We might call it a reaction, but it is more measured and purposeful than that.

The second thing of engagement is a *moment*

When we respond to something it happens in a moment of time, in contrast to the timeless, ongoing nature of scattering a message. Responding is often the product of thought and time, but when it happens, it is a definitive moment of action and of interaction. Every time you go to your local café you are gathering around them in a moment of time. Their message is constantly displayed on their signage, by their presence on the street, by the chairs outside, but when you walk into it and make your order it is a specific moment in time in which you respond to the message.

Commerce in particular is driven by moments. Like with the coffee shop, we constantly browse websites and walk past stores that are messaging to us, but it is the moment that we click or walk in the store and make the purchase that is the moment we transition from receiver to responder, and from punter to customer.

It's between *initiator* and *responder*

In the Gather process a receiver transitions to being a *responder*, for by responding they have said, "I wish to engage with this", and have gathered themselves to the initiator, ceasing to merely be a receiver. It is the other half to stimulus-response theory.

A responder is more active than a receiver. To receive something can be a largely passive act, but to respond to something involves a moment of action. It is here that participation begins with the message. To go back to our Lord of the Rings conversation analogy with Fred and Sally, it's when Sally not only acknowledges that Fred has started talking about literature, which she loves; it's now that she responds, and enthusiastically so at that!

There is is also an important distinction between a response and a reaction. A response is to the initiator, but a reaction is within one's self. Someone might see an advert and feel put off by it, maybe even repulsed, but that's a reaction that remains inside that person, and certainly without any response to the advert that signals more engagement. We'll come back to this later in the book, but it's important to flag it now.

The difference between response and reaction also helps to understand the imperative of this second process within the Circle of Engagement:

The moment should be a *gathering!*

Fred had originally tried to talk with Sally about The Beatles, but it later turned out that Lord of the Rings was the thing that Sally really responded to. It behooved Fred, of course, to then pick up on that and talk more about that topic. Sally didn't just react, she responded. She participated. She engaged back with Fred.

In the same way, when people respond to us, it is an opportunity to engage more with them, and we will achieve more engagement if we gather in that moment around their response and a topic of shared interest, rather that just our own interest. We will have bigger intentions for our relationship than this current conversation, but let us lay that aside for a moment and remember we are on a journey, and the imperative at this point is to engage at this level of response, and then point to where we can go next.

Think of how some websites celebrate the moment someone has made a purchase (rather than trying to instantly sell them more), how teams do better when they are focussed in their meeting, and how a political leader when visiting a place should pay attention to the needs of the person in front of them rather than just canvas a vote. If we do the part of focussing and gathering, the rest will come. In other words, the better we Gather, the better we'll Matter, as we'll see shortly.

There is also a second way responders gather: to each other, which is something with exponential power. This is the network effect, where an entity is more valuable the more that people use it.

Peer gathering forms a triangle of connection: far more durable and resilient than a sole two-way connection between the initiator and a single responder. The social identity that is created when these people gather did not exist before hand, and whilst it can be facilitated, it is not the creation of any one party, and can't happen without togetherness.

And you?

- When have you responded to a message today? How has that response been a moment of interaction? Think about how specific a moment it was, whether it was tactile, and what your response to it was.
- When are the moments of interaction that you have with your customers, employees and/or community members?
- Does your organisation gather responders to each other? If so, how? Are those people more engaged as a result?

Matter

Whenever something goes beyond informing, entertaining, or supplying us, and fulfils the role of enabling us, they have gone from providing something briefly engaging to something that fosters long-term engagement. Things that enable us are things that matter to us and things that stick with us: it's the meal that the farmer's crop produces, the deep conversations that truly connect people, or the social network that connects friends and families across the globe.

If we want to build an enduring connection then we will need to understand what it is to matter to someone, and what this third process does that is distinct to the previous two.

The third thing of engagement is *means and meaning*

Things that matter provide us the means to do more in our lives. The Matter process takes what has been gathered, and turns that into a lasting resource with benefit and utility. The tangible things that matter provide us with *means*. Our cars are means, and are products we are highly engaged with! So too are our jobs as means for our life, or our phones as means to stay in contact with friends and family, or the gym as a means to stay fit. If we think back to our farming analogy, the means is the food, as it's a means to being nourished and fed.

But in the case of the conversation analogy, there was something more. After the conversation, Fred and Sally had developed a bond. This is not means, but *meaning*.

People who attend church or another religious service are engaging with meaning. So too are people who pick one brand over another because they identify more strongly with that brand as it has greater meaning to them. That is actually what loyalty to a brand often is: loyalty to the meaning that one derives from that brand. It also works in an employee and team context. The teams we love to be part of give us meaning, purpose and mission, and from that we can derive a sense of identity and direction.

It's between *initiator* **and** *cooperator*

In the Matter process the receiver-turned-responder makes another transition, their final one, into *cooperator*. They have gone responding *to* the organisation, to acting *with* the organisation. They make use of the means and meaning, applying them to their own life, and advocating for them so that others can encounter them too.

By calling this person the cooperator we really are emphasising that the relationship has become one of partnership. The cooperator has ownership of this relationship. They engage in just as much as the initiator does, and sometimes even more.

The means should matter!

It could be said that we're all highly engaged by the supermarkets we shop at, because they give us one of the most important means of all: food! Yet most people would not discriminate between which supermarket they go to, opting mostly for which is the most convenient at the time they need something.

So why is it that it provides us means, but it doesn't really matter to us? Because for something to matter to us it must provide both the means and the meaning. And I think you'd agree, rarely can we call one of our grocery shops a meaningful experience!

We will have had many conversations with people, but it is those conversations that made a difference, that were meaningful, that took our relationship with someone to a deeper level, that we would say had *mattered*. It's the same with the other entities we engage with, such as our work, the products and services we use, and the communities we belong to: we have enduring connections with those things that matter to us through means and meaning.

I find business books an interesting entry here. Most business books endeavour to communicate an idea or framework as a means that is memorable and usable so that it enable better decision making, provides a world view that gives its readers a sense of meaning and purpose, and aids their own journey existentially and practically. If a book, video, talk, or perhaps even a film, song, or novel has ever changed the way you think for the better, you know what it is to be enabled by something that provides means and meaning. Think about the song lyric that at first was just scattered, that you then gathered around, and now has become a deeply meaningful phrase that matters to you.

In the conversation analogy, it's because the idea that Fred and Sally were discussing was so engaging that they chatted about it again. When things matter to us, they connect us, and we engage again, which is why it feeds back into the Scatter process.

And you?

- What provides means and meaning in your life, both personal and professional? For example, think about software and tools, world views, what you read or watch, and the spaces you inhabit.

- What means does your organisation provide that matter to your customers, employees and community members? How do they cooperator with your means?

- Do you provide a sense of meaning as well as means? If not, why might it be that your meaning isn't getting through?

The Iterating Cycle of Engagement

We've used the metaphor of farming to show how the Matter process, in this case the wheat, has within it the seed to start the Scatter process again. It's the same within the Circle of Engagement.

However when we engage with someone a second time, it's not the same as the first. Because of our previous engagement, we begin this second one in an elevated position, with a win under our belt as it were. It's the difference between the first time you meet someone, and the second. We don't meet someone for the second time and yet go through the process as if it were the first, asking what their name is and what they spend their time doing –we've already established that, and use that conversation as the foundation to build the second.

To illustrate this, let's look at the *Iterating Cycle of Engagement*. When one cycle of Scatter, Gather, Matter is completed, another begins, albeit because there is now a platform that matters between the two parties, they start from an elevated position. We could plot the process as *Scatter > Gather > Matter > Scatter > Gather > Matter* and so on, each circle increasing the value of the relationship.

The Iterating Cycle of Engagement

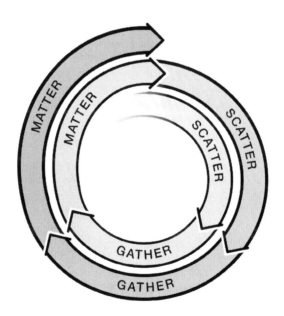

A parent or teacher will readily appreciate this as a visual for the lessons they have taught their children or pupils. New lessons are taught based on what has been learned in previous lessons. Each lesson serves to uphold the others, and at other times when those things which matter are returned to, they become norms, then habits, and then beliefs. It is in this way that parents aim to instil into their children values, and is indeed the way we learn anything.

The key word here is platform. When something matters it provides a platform, a stage, a higher level of ground, which elevates the relationship.

In particular, a platform elevates people above certain obstacles and provides certain new abilities, and thus enables them to do more in their life. If we consider a conversation again, a second conversation has been elevated above the obstacle of getting to know some core facts – as this was done in the first conversation.

The products we use that matter to us have an elevated relationship with us compared to the products that don't matter to us. In some cases, they are building on years of loyalty as a platform, which is a good indicator of our ongoing loyalty to them.

Platform is also an increasingly popular business model in two-sided business models, where marketplaces of networks of people come together.

For Apple and Android, this meant creating a marketplace where users could overcome the obstacle of finding the right apps, and app developers could overcome the obstacle of reaching their customers; so that those obstacles no longer existed. Both Apple and Android gathered their developers and users – not just to themselves, but to each other – and now have turned that resource into a platform: something that truly matters to hundreds of millions of people.

The maxim for platform is that it enables us to do things we couldn't do before, and now can't do without; whether that's the prior conversations that our current relationship is built on, the phone we use to do new things we couldn't before, or our workplace that has greatly enabled our professional and personal life through great work and good pay.

And you?

- What brand or product has slowly built a relationship with you through a series of Scatter, Gather, Matter cycles? For ideas, look to what entities you have an exclusive relationship with, such as the same car manufacturer, your regular café, or handheld device of choice.

- How do your customers, employees, and communities build on the platform that you provide? Can you spot how the loop iterates?

- Or is it a frustration that your organisation doesn't seem to build on engagement, but instead lets it slip away?

* * *

The Circle of Engagement • Reference Table

Process	What it is	Initiator and	Direction
Scatter	Message	Receiver	Out
Gather	Moment	Responder	In
Matter	Means & Meaning	Cooperator	Up

O V E 4 * X &

V

The Engage-Vent

Why is a click not engagement?

Here's a question that has plagued me for years:

At what point can we say something *is* engagement, and what point is something *not* engagement?

To establish the importance of this question, let us look briefly at social media. According to Facebook's terminology at the time of writing, a like, comment, click or share of a post are all put under the metric of 'engagement', as opposed to how many have seen the post, which is the 'reach' metric. This is problematic. A 'like' is somewhat different to a comment, which is different to watching a video, which is different again to clicking on a link, all of which are click actions in themselves of one kind or another. Furthermore, as I will argue in this shape, *none* of these clicks are actually engagement, they are merely interactions!

This isn't just limited to Facebook. Many engagement practitioners feel frustrated by the view from management that a click – things like filling in a survey, sending an email asking a question, liking a post, or posting a letter – are considered to be engagement. It's merely a checkbox exercise that says "Tick! Engagement is done!"

And of course, it has *not* been done. The danger of treating a click as engagement is that it creates the illusion that engagement has happened when it hasn't, and worse still, by lumping everything into one pot we lose our strategic discernment to treat different activities differently.

Our task in this shape is to unpick this mess of metrics and define what are the units of engagement. Thus enter the Engage-Vent, and our second shape.

V

The Engage-Vent is like a funnel, the V on your keyboard (think V for Vent!). It's also a pun that I just couldn't resist: engage-*ment* and engage-*vent* sound rather alike, or at least I think so! Just like a funnel or a vent, this model is a flow of relationship activity. Plus, it allows me to 'give vent' to my frustration that a click isn't engagement, damnit!

The V shape shows how relationship has different building blocks, from the sharp point at the bottom (which is the precise moment of action), to the broad, open ended top (which is the potential of the relationship).

On the left of the V are the units of relationship, the smallest at the bottom, and the largest at the top. On the right is what the unit needs to go from and to, i.e. from coincidental interaction to consistent interaction.

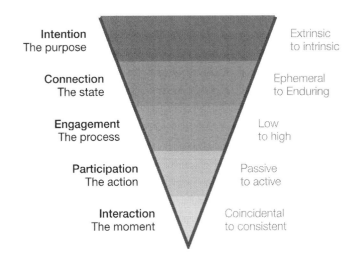

Intention The purpose	Extrinsic to intrinsic
Connection The state	Ephemeral to Enduring
Engagement The process	Low to high
Participation The action	Passive to active
Interaction The moment	Coincidental to consistent

Interaction

I've just slammed the notion that a click is engagement. So where in a relationship does the click fall? Here. A click is an interaction. It's the exact moment when a button is pressed, a survey filled in, an email responded to, a product bought, an invitation made to go on a date, the moment someone says 'yes', a keyboard stroke, click of a mouse, and other highly practical, tangible actions.

Interaction is the *moment* of relationship

It is the smallest, most tangible unit of engagement. It's the part of relationship that we can put our finger on the most, such as when someone says something, or when we notice someone does *not* say something, or when we see an advert, or when a store clerk speaks to us, or when we open the app on our phone.

Interaction is not engagement itself, rather engagement is built on layers of interaction. Interaction is the most precise unit, and it is also the most voluminous. There are dozens of moments of interactions within the broader action of participation, which is the next unit up. If I am invited to fill in a survey, I receive the invitation, I open it up, I think about it, I fill it in (while still thinking about it), I send it, I continue to think about it afterward. All of this is participation. But the precise moments in time when I open, fill it in, and click 'send', are the interactions.

Transition from *coincidental* to *consistent interaction*

For the unengaged, opening, clicking, responding, buying, attending, performing and the like will only ever be *coincidental interaction*. Furthermore, there is no frequency or mechanism to make interactions with them more predictable in the first place.

The engaged, on the other hand, because the relationship is so strong, and habits have been so well developed, enjoy *consistent interaction* that is rhythmic and predictable with the entity. Think of the average person who is highly engaged with their phone. They consistently interact with it, and once you become an app on their home screen, you can take advantage of the consistency of sight.

And you?

- What are the interactions your organisation has with those that it is engaging? Think back to the Gather process for ideas.
- Are your interactions fairly consistent? Or do you find that they are more coincidental? How does this impact your ability to engage?
- Do you call things 'engagement' that are actually interactions?

Participation

It wasn't long after I started writing about engagement in 2009 that I quickly discovered its brother-in-arms, participation. For many people, these terms are synonymous, however, I have found that participation speaks more to action than it does to emotions, process or the state of a relationship. We can find a film very engaging, but would not say it was very participatory.

In a social sense, and writing at the time as an events producer, I said that *participation is the currency of engagement*. Years later, I still stand by that. Let's unpack it:

Participation is the *action* of relationship

Interaction is the series of moments that create participation. For instance, every word spoken in a conversation is an interaction. But the conversation itself is the participation, unless someone stops participating, of course.

Engagement, the process of making the most of a relationship, happens because we are participating, which happens because there is interaction.

Transition from *passive* to *active participation*

The unengaged only act with *passive participation*. For instance, a political party looks to create participation through debates and town hall meetings. If an individual is only passively or thinly participating in the election from home, that will likely be the height of it, and their vote will almost certainly be determined by generational or relational influence rather than being informed by their own research and interaction with the party. But if they can get that individual to participate in some way by acting: attending a debate maybe, even if only watching it, then they have a chance of engaging them.

By contrast, the highly engaged *actively participate*. By virtue of being emotionally involved they are also behaviourally involved, informing themselves through research, debating with friends, advocating in a range of forms, and maybe volunteering and being part of a street team. Such people regularly support others, transitioning from being consumers to becoming creators and carers, a desirable change in any engagement context.

On a local government level where there is not a vote to be won, this level of participation is still enviable. Having the involvement of local people in a community issue such as infrastructure, health or education helps foster buy-in, soothe contentions, and ensures that voices are heard.

To conclude, we could say that engagement is evidenced by participation, but that we need to create participation if we want engagement. Which leads us to the E-word itself…

And you?

- Who or what are you personally participating with at the moment? Can you spot how many interactions fit into one act of participation?

- Within your organisation, is the participation generally passive, which results in you being frustrated with low responses? Or is participation generally active? If so, why?

Engagement

In the Prologue, I defined engagement as the process of making the most of a relationship. But contrary to what many might think, and perhaps ironically as this is a book about engagement, engagement is not an end in itself. Engagement is the means by which the end is achieved, or perhaps more helpfully, the *process* by which a relationship is built.

Engagement is the *process* of relationship

The etymology of the word is the French to *interlock* or to *commit*, derived from the gauntlet that a knight would throw down to signal a challenge, and then later use in the challenge. It is a coming together, an active interlocking, of two entities (whether people, ideas or products) over a certain period of time.

The length of time is not set, but it is a period of time in which both parties are generally actively participating. Engagement cannot happen when there is inactivity for too long a period: by definition, once the two parties unlock, the engagement is over, but hopefully, a connection has been built that transcends inaction.

Transition from *low* to *high engagement*

Initially people "need a reason" to engage that provides a clear benefit. While this is expected for the beginning of a relationship, the unengaged remain like this, and will only ever engage with what they deem as having clear reasons and benefits. They have *low engagement*. This is suitable for those who do not require a high level of engagement, but for those organisations who want to foster trust, loyalty, and achieve innovative things, they need relationship to be the basis on which they engage.

The engaged have not forgone reason, but they have added relationship to it, and thus are willing to do things because they "have a relationship" that the unengaged would not, such as try new products, put in more hours, or volunteer, when there aren't clear benefits or there is a risk attached. Such people have *high engagement*, are loyal to the relationship, and are willing to overlook failure, fault and even harm to certain extents.

- Is there a particular thing your organisation is 'interlocking' and engaging with people on at the moment?

- Can you think of the customers, employees and members who only engage with you if they have a reason to, and those who engage because they have a relationship with you? What's the difference in terms of your effort to provide value to them?

Connection

To achieve the intention of the engagement, there must be a bond between the parties involved. The aim of engagement, therefore, is to build a state of connection that outlasts time and periods of inaction, proportional to the intention of the relationship.

It's impractical to be constantly engaging people: we have lives to live, and also need times at slower pace. But it is a different thing to have an enduring connection that sits over engagement.

Connection is the *state* of relationship

Two friends who have not spoken in years have, by definition, not engaged with each other during that time. Yet their connection is a state that is stronger than the lack of a recent process of engagement. It is the same principle for marriage, partnerships, and parenthood, where the bond of connection transcends the ups and downs of family relations. A child might be disengaged in the family, but still be connected to the family. Disconnection would be far more painful than disengagement.

Likewise, an employee who is usually engaged in their work may find themselves unengaged with a particular project, yet their connection to the organisation is such that this temporary dip in engagement does not affect their overall productivity and commitment.

Thus, connection is a state. Whilst it is not visible, its presence is certainly felt.

Transition from *ephemeral* to *enduring connection*

When the relationship with the unengaged is subject to coincidental interaction, such as their passing by a store at a certain time of day, or seeing an advert, there will only be an *ephemeral connection* with the entity. Additionally, such a person is being competed for by a range of brands, and their purchasing decisions will likely be determined by the roll of the coincidence dice.

The engaged on the other hand have *enduring connections* with brands that ensure their loyalty remains even through periods of apparent low spending. They have a bond with the brand that will lead them to hold out on a phone upgrade in order to wait for the next phone release, even if it's a year away. A customer may have a connection to a particular trainer, watch or car brand for which they have lifetime loyalty to the exclusion of other, perhaps more convenient, brand offerings. The connection is deep: it has become a matter of the 'heart' rather than of the 'head'.

This connection also affects key associated areas such as retention, loyalty, investment, churn, advocacy, and frequency of use or spend, because the bond they have is stronger than temporal distractions, allures or frustrations.

And you?

- Think about a friend who you are connected to, even though you haven't engaged with them recently. Why does your connection transcend the lack of regular engagement?

- Are there people that have an enduring connection with your organisation? How did that come to be? Think about what messages, moments, means and meaning are involved.

- What would someone who is connected to your organisation describe themselves as?

Intention

Any relationship has an intention and a purpose. With friends and family that purpose is enjoyment and support of each other, which takes precedence over any other intention. Within customer, employee, and community engagement, it's about the intentions of both the initiator, and the receiver. In work, the purpose is to do the job, and whilst friends are made and organisations enable their employees in many ways, that purpose is the intention for all that flows between employer and employee. At a café the staff can build up a friendly rapport with their customers, even be supportive of them, but don't be confused: the intention of both parties is still primarily one of purchasing and enjoying a coffee.

Intention is the thread that runs through every part of the relationship, through connection, engagement, participation, and down to interaction. They all point to the intention. To use a British idiom, intention is the "writing through the stick of rock."

Intention is the *purpose* of relationship

Engagement is not the goal of a relationship. The idea of being engaged to be married, or engaged for a consulting project or speaking appointment, illustrates how engagement denotes intention towards something larger. Intention points towards the true purpose of the relationship.

If we return to engagement at work for a moment, and consider employee engagement, having engaged employees is not actually the purpose. As much as being engaged in one's work is a benefit in and of itself for employer and employee alike, it is not the end for either of them. An employer has a broader intention of what to achieve with that engagement, (most likely, it's corporate purpose and mission), and likewise, an employee, while they enjoy being engaged in their work, has intentions around the whole of their life. Indeed, it is actually because of intention that engagement occurs.

Turning to the community engagement space, it was the goal of racial equality that engaged people in the civil rights movement, not vice-versus. Thus the broad, open-ended top of the V represents the range of intentions that one can have when looking to engage with another entity.

Transition from *extrinsic* to *intrinsic intention*

One major hallmark of the engaged is the source of their motivation towards the entity they are engaged with. The unengaged, being subject to coincidence, need the *extrinsic intention* of that coincidence to resonate with their own intention in order to bring about a transaction, whether that be purchasing, volunteering, putting in extra on a project, and so forth.

The engaged however are beyond being buyers: they are believers. This religious language is fitting. An engaged member of a religion has moved from the external motivation in the form of exhortations from their minister to *intrinsic intention* that comes from a conviction about core beliefs and truths. They do not need the prompting of their minister to pray, to donate, to invite friends and family: they desire to do it themselves.

We could say that the engaged self-serve. The engaged employee will ask for help when they need it, find the resources when they don't have them, and not wait for a boss to motivate them. They simply do not need as many cues from an initiator as the unengaged do, thus saving expense and effort, and increasing productivity for the organisation. An engaged customer will likewise take solving their product issues into their own hands, and bear with the product, even when support might not be forthcoming.

And you?

- Think back to a time that you had to motivate an unengaged person. Compare this with someone who was engaged and therefore intrinsically motivated. What was the difference in outcome?

- What is your organisation's intention? Is your engagement working toward that? Think about things like your vision, mission, purpose, goals, and objectives.

Flipping the Funnel

So Interaction is the most precise unit, with each unit being broader in the time which it inhabits. It's a funnel, where Intention seeps down into the very moment of Interaction.

Yet, if we flip the the Engage-Vent, we'll discover that it's also a pyramid of activity. There is a large base, say dozens, of interactions, which fuel several participatory actions. These active participations feed a few times of high engagement. These processes of engagement, each one as a new Scatter, Gather, Matter cycle increasing in value and resonance, is feeding maybe two or three emotional connections that the subject of the engagement has: one with the initiator, one with other responders, and maybe another nuanced connection with a particular offering from the initiator. These connections, as emotional states, help both parties to achieve their respective current intentions, until of course those are fulfilled, and new ones take pole position.

The Flipped Engage-Vent

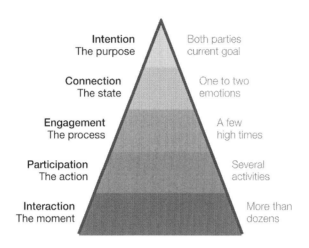

Intention The purpose	Both parties current goal
Connection The state	One to two emotions
Engagement The process	A few high times
Participation The action	Several activities
Interaction The moment	More than dozens

And you?

- Can you see within your own organisation how many interactions are building participation, which is building engagement, and so on, up to fulfilling your intention?
- Could you audit those to create an engagement strategy?

* * *

The Engage-Vent • Reference Table

Unit	What it is	From	To
Interaction	Moment	Coincidental	Consistent
Participation	Action	Passive	Active
Engagement	Process	Low	High
Connection	State	Ephemeral	Enduring
Intention	Purpose	Extrinsic	Intrinsic

OVE4✳X&

E

The 3-E Maturity Model

What is the level of your engagement?

Not all engagement is equal.

Our everyday dialogue gives it away: somethings are *very engaging*, others *quite engaging* or maybe *not very engaging*, whereas something else might be *incredibly engaging*. This is no surprise.

An advert that engaged us, and we can recall it when discussing it with friends, hardly compares to an idea that has engaged us and changed the way we think. And this is different again from the technology that we use every day that is engaging in a different way again.

This isn't just because there are different *intensities* of engagement, like two theatre shows that differ in how engaging the experience is. It's because there are different *levels* of engagement.

Imagine therefore that we took the Circle of Engagement and rolled it out in a straight line. I'm sure you've already cottoned on that the three processes of *Scatter > Gather > Matter* represent three distinct maturities of engagement.

Scatter as the first process is all about communicating the message. If the message can be engaged with, because one can receive and respond to it in some way, like seeing an advert and buying because of it, then the message itself is an engagement offering. We'll call this level Engagement as *Expression*.

Gather is the second process and is about creating a moment. It's experiential and focussed on interaction and participation. Where one can engage with an experience when they respond, that's a second level: Engagement as *Experience*.

Matter is the third and final process from the Cycle of Engagement, and as we know, is about providing means and meaning. When someone can engage as a cooperator, and benefit from means and meanings, we are at the third and final level of maturity: Engagement as *Enablement*.

E

The 3-E Maturity Model is easy to remember because it's the letter E, and they relate to three maturities, each beginning with an E, relating to the three prongs on the letter.

On the single vertical line of the letter we have the three processes, Scatter, Gather and Matter. They sit next to the three prongs, each prong representing a process and the maturity of its offering, as we've described above.

The lowest maturity goes first, up to the highest. Each level is progressive, building on the previous one.

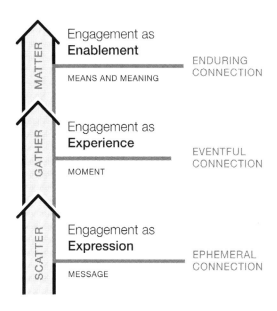

Engagement as Expression

The most frequent thing that we engage with as humans is expression. Someone puts out a message. Sometimes we receive it. Sometimes we react to it. Sometimes, we also respond to it. But what is certain is that messages of every kind are being scattered at every moment, and this currency of engagement is by far the most popular. Some estimates put this at 90% of what comprises engagement. Some engagement will go higher, but regardless, it all starts here.

Engagement as Expression is where engagement occurs around the message. Music, adverts, media, emails, tweets, posters, requests – they are all expressions of a message.

As we've said, all engagement begins here, and it is often down to how the receiver resonates with the message, and whether they become a responder or cooperator, that determines if the organisation can go onto a higher level of engagement.

However some organisations are happy to remain here. This isn't to say that they do not have more than a message to offer as far as engagement goes; they might well do, but it is not pursued.

Many consumer commodities rightly operate only at this level of engagement. Most drivers will purchase fuel based on the expression of price, not the experience of the station. Many products within supermarkets likewise are purchased solely on expression of price and with the job to be done in mind. I recall a personal occasion where a bleach had been branded as a "Special Spring Edition", but this was expecting too much engagement. I was not in the mind to experience a special edition of a bleach: I solely wanted the one that was the cheapest for the job that needed to be done. Likewise, an internal company memo that updates employees on a project's progress without needing any further interaction is suitable for just expression and no higher form of engagement (although, we will still want that memo to be spreadable, of course).

It is dependant on the *communications* capability

To deliver Engagement as Expression, organisations must be able to communicate their message. This clearly rests within the functions and departments of communications (internal and external), marketing, PR, and advertising.

And the better they can communicate their message, the better engagement they can expect. Accordingly, there are some key considerations and implications:

Firstly, clear and consistent communication wins the day. The most inspiring communicators, grandest ideas, and greatest offerings, if inconsistently communicated, will not succeed. Within my work as an advisor on engagement strategy I have all too often found that quality was lost in inconsistency. One key reason is that we're talking about the Scatter process here. Going back to our farming analogy, a farmer has to be pretty darn consistent to get their harvest – that's the nature of seed – you just don't know which is going to bear fruit, and which isn't. Consistency ensures you are giving every seed of a message the best chance for success.

Additionally, whether one is only offering Engagement as Expression, or if they intend to further their engagement, communication is the foundational capability. The higher levels of engagement cannot make up for poor communications. If the foundation is off, the whole building will be off.

Another consideration is the increasing multiplicity of channels. Gone are the days where an article in the paper and an email round robin did the trick. Today our receivers, responders, and cooperators dwell in diverse channels, yet each expects that channel to grant them access. To express well, a range of online and offline tactics must be embraced.

The sensibility is to *create* something *spreadable*

In light of the diversity of channels at our disposal (or peril, depending on your view!), the best messages are those that can be adapted to each channel, and foster word of mouth so that they spread from person to person.

To achieve this, these messages should be spreadable by design. The stronger an organisation's ability to create compelling messaging, and create the most opportunity for it to spread, the better they will fare.

Within a digital marketing context, this could clearly displaying social media share buttons. Television adverts are often spreadable based on jingles and catch phrases. Memes spread through their novelty. Impactful ideas often spread through memorable metaphors and clever turns of phrase, such as *"I have a dream"*, or *"Red sky at night, shepherd's delight; red sky in the morning, shepherd's warning."*

It is a *childlike* level of maturity

This is not to minimise its importance, for this is the starting point of all engagement, but rather highlight the distinctive factors of childlikeness; namely being those things that are developed within an organisation's infancy, and those things which as an engagement device are about direction and outbound communication, much like a parent-child relationship. There is indeed also a negative element: a child is more likely to be unaware of what resonates with others, because it is focussed on its own interests, like the software developer who might fail to translate the features they find so fascinating into benefits that actually enrich the end user. A child is also easily distracted, which is why many organisations have taken to over-messaging, as we've described above.

As you'd expect, a message is only briefly engaging, unless it progresses to be a message that is experienced or enabling. Because it is so ephemeral and fleeting, one must keep expressing to keep people engaged, and ensure it is accessible and available as broadly as possible. The receivers of the engagement are consumers of what the initiator creates, and the initiator must keep on creating. It is because of this that we experience a proliferation of advertising, which has led to its unwanted cousins, spam email and interruption marketing. But such desperate tactics are needed when a receiver is only engaged when receiving a message. Additionally, yesterday's expression is not today's expression. Organisations who exist at this maturity level have to compete with the customer's desire for the new and novel, and the many others vying for their eyeballs. This is why many voices, including mine, are urging organisations to take up the challenge to engage at higher levels in order to build deeper connections.

And you?

- Engagement as Expression is very common, and can be very enjoyable: such as music, a newsletter, or advertisement. But what are the disadvantages of only engaging with a message, and no further?
- How engaging is your expression? Think about consistency, spreadability, and accessibility.

Engagement as Experience

In the second process of engagement the initiator and responders come together in a shared moment of time, gathering around each other. Such activity is the offering of experience.

Engagement as Experience is where people engage for the gathering experience. Initiators at this level of maturity will be those organisations that can get an audience, bring people together, and even deliver a powerful moment. This could be an event, an app, a store, a theme park: anything that is interaction within a specific moment of time.

This is a suitable level of engagement to operate at where the offering is solely an experience. As an example, Broadway musicals know a customer will attend a show once, maybe twice at most in their lifetime. Hopefully they will sell various memorabilia to the customer, but beyond that, there is no further engagement that they can provide to the customer that they would otherwise wish to have. The customer is ostensibly looking for an experience from the show, not enablement of wider life fulfilment.

It is dependant on the *experience staging* capability

Entities at this level of maturity are reliably staging experiences that provide first hand interaction between parties, such as retail stores, conferences and events, leisure activities, venues and places, and products themselves that are highly interactive and tactile, such as certain vehicles, lifestyle utilities, digital devices and apps. As a specific moment in time, in retail, gathering is what happens when a customer comes into the store. For an app, it's when someone uses their app (often multiple times a day). For a relationship, it's when someone agrees to join you on a date. For an employee, it's when people show up on a project, signalling their buy-in and commitment.

On the topic of what offering is provided at this level, a potential point of confusion could surround publications, such as newspapers, magazines, and email newsletters, as they are ostensibly an offering of communication. Are these just the first level of Engagement as Expression? They can be, but often they move into this second level of maturity of Engagement as Experience because the act of reading them is an experience, an interaction, shared between the publication and the reader. There are often rituals involved around daily or weekend newspapers, reading while commuting, taking a magazine to a coffee shop, done by people who have chosen to subscribe to a certain publication over another, and as we'll see in Shape 6, derive identity from that interaction, and would be loathe to give it up.

The sensibility is to *co-create* by being *shareable*

To enable high levels of experience and identity formation, an experience needs to be richly and interactively shared in. If this is a concert, the crowd want to sing along. If it's a retail store, the customer wants to interact with the products and try them out, so that they can imagine their identity if they owned them. With a project group, people want to contribute what they do best (which might not be speaking up in a meeting, but instead be putting things into action with speed and precision).

To achieve this, unlike the Scatter process which emphasises creation ability, the Gather process, where the maturity is experience, emphasises co-creation ability. What determines how engaging an experience is will be the degree to which the responder can indeed respond to it and share in it.

When initiator and responder come together in a moment, that moment itself is co-created by both parties. If one of them were missing, the moment would not happen. Where responders also gather to each other as well as to the initiator, the moment is co-created not just by two but by *many* parties. The more that people can co-create the moment, share in it, be immersed in it, contribute to it, the more engaging it will prove to be as a moment.

It's a tautology, and perhaps blatantly obvious, but the more engaging (verb) something is, the more engaging (adjective) it is, or vice verses!

Thus the door must be wide open to sharing. Facilitating a high degree of co-creation like this often does not require clever strategies. Rather, if the basics are done well, and people are given a chance to get involved at the level they'd like, the initiator has done sufficient to encourage a rich co-creative experience. There is also a hidden benefit to co-creative experiences. The mantra of the responder is 'If I can share in it, I'll share it', which is why we find people tend to share with others what they have a part in.

It is a *teenage* level of maturity

The teenager years are marked by sensory experience, social interaction, and personal exploration as the individual transitions from a child to an adult with a formed sense of identity. Fittingly, this is the place of experiences, and as we've discussed in the *Circle of Engagement*, the place where social identity can be co-created. Negatively, this can be a fickle level: whilst it is valued by the sensory high of the experience, it is easily forsaken when a new or better high comes along.

The onus is not on whether the company is putting out its message (which can interrupt its receivers to a certain degree), but on whether the receiver becomes a responder and gathers to the company. This puts the control firmly in the hands of the responder. If they are not motivated to continue experiencing the initiator, whether that be the product, their workplace, a community, an event, a speaker, then they will vote with their feet, and the engagement will end.

Whereas many organisations should have no need to move onto the third and final level of maturity because their offering is an experience, they are finding that engagement fades, and they must work harder to achieve the same engagement next time round. Additionally, the challenge presented by an increasing number of competitors is a commanding reason for them to consider going beyond engagement as experience.

And you?

• Do you offer a shareable experience? Can your customers, employees and communities co-create with you?

- What Engagement as Experience do your competitors provide? Are you meeting the rising demand of experiences as economic offerings?

- How could you make people's interactions with you – whether in person, physical or digital – an experience as opposed to just an expression?

Engagement as Enablement

Expression is what is pushed out to the receiver. Experience is what the responder chooses to gather around. But beyond the brevity of a message or the temporal high of an experience, there is a form of engagement that is long-lasting and life changing.

This is Engagement as Enablement. This level is about mattering to people by providing a platform and resources that can be used to live a better life. These users were receivers, who became responders, and now they are cooperators, using the platform to enable and enhance their work, their enjoyment, their family, and their life.

It is dependant on the *platform delivery* capability

Platform is a business model that is receiving more and more attention as ecosystems of offerings have filled the foreground of our lives as consumers. The growth of major social media platforms over the last 20 years is indicative of the trend towards this. Facebook enables people to connect with friends in a way they couldn't before, and it enables businesses to offer their services to targeted groups in a way they previously couldn't. Google Adwords enabled marketers by eliminating the need to know where to market: they were all there on Google, you just needed to use the platform. Amazon has eliminated the need for many authors (including this one) to find a traditional publisher, and instead enables us to self publish with speed, ease and at no cost.

However platforms are not only provided by technology firms. A school is a platform. A bar, café or pub can be a platform to its regulars. Lifestyle, religious, political or other core life beliefs provide a platform for us to build further worldviews and ideas on.

Whether one calls it a platform, a community, a tool, a network, or marketplace, or even a non-tangible platform, such as an idea or concept that enables people, these are all lasting resources that give means and meaning.

The sensibility is to *procreate* by being *scaleable*

The best platforms are those which scale with the end user. Consider the product that keeps improving, such as software updates, or the philosophical and religious ideas that seem to get deeper the more one looks into them. When more people access a platform, and its scale increases, it enjoys regular iterations of the Scatter, Gather, Matter loop, where satisfied cooperators spread the message further and further afield.

There has been *creation* of a message, and *co-creation* with the experience, but this process is one of *procreation* through the platform and the means and meaning. Quite literally, when one becomes a cooperator with Engagement as Enablement, then that platform of enabling allows them to procreate new things in their life that they could not without the platform.

Consider how our devices enable us to create our own things with them. In an employee context, consider how a company that offers home working and flexible hours enables those employees to live richer home lives, particularly pertinent if they have children. Such employees will become advocates for the company, and return the gift of enablement with their own gift of commitment to the organisation. Or look at how communities enable members to fulfil their ambitions through the means and meaning they provide: each fulfilment being something procreated through or because of the platform.

It is *adulthood* in its level of maturity

Adults carry responsibility, reproduce, provide for the needs of their children, and have their working life to consider, a clear progression from the thrill-seeking teenager. Engagement as Enablement reflects this: it too has grown up and is more concerned about actualised value than temporary fascination.

But whilst these platforms are adept at fostering mature engagement, they cannot stand still. People will engage with them, but only as long as they enable them. Competitors abound, and inertia always seeks to slow adoption, usage, and involvement down. And without highly engaged users, staff, members or the like, a platform will crumble as it does not have the network effect that grants it its true value. Thus even the most popular of platforms must keep on engaging, and keep on innovating.

This also rings true for non-tangible platforms. Rare are the ideas that come into our lives and stay for the entirety of them. Most provide benefit for a season before they are replaced by new ideas. The skill of crafting an idea to update itself is a discerning skill indeed.

And you?

- What can people do because of the Engagement as Enablement that you provide?

- Think about what things personally enable you on a daily basis. How many are there? Consider products, ideas, relationships, tools, networks, and the like.

* * *

The 3-E Maturity Model • Reference Table

Level	Maturity	Process	Capability	Sensibility
Expression	Childlike	Scatter	Communication	Spreadable
Experience	Teenage	Gather	Experience	Shareable
Enablement	Adulthood	Matter	Platform	Scaleable

OVE4✶X&

4

The 4-and-a-half Frontiers of Engagement

Who is engaging with whom?

One of the things that can be confusing about engagement is the various contexts in which the word is used.

Its technical use spans back decades, and over time has developed into at least four distinct professional disciplines. I call these the *Frontiers of Engagement*, for though the ideas that engagement encapsulates are as old as time, their focussed implementation in the working world is recent, gaining increased notoriety over the last decade in tandem with the rise of social media and the increasing democratisation of access and capability. Trends such as flat organisations, disruptive peer to peer technologies, social media fuelled revolutions, and personal followings as a norm are undoubtably signs of a faster, person-to-person world where hierarchy has given way to effectiveness.

It is no surprise that this is all happening over the same period in history that humanity is, in general, becoming more tolerant of one another. Thus, those working in engagement are indeed on a frontier. They are developing new norms, innovating with human relationship, and shaping best practices that others will follow, often in opposition or at least disruption to what went before.

4

The 4-and-a-half Frontiers of Engagement are conveniently represented by the shape of the number 4 itself. The vertical and horizontal lines form a 2x2 matrix: the top right, bottom right, and bottom left quadrants are the three main recognised professions of engagement that I've referred to throughout the book; *customer*, *employee*, and *community* engagement.

The top left quadrant is marked by the diagonal line that really makes this shape a number 4, and not just a peculiar cross. It's this quadrant that accounts for the fourth frontier of engagement and the extra half. These are the 'personal' spaces of *interpersonal* and *intrapersonal* engagement.

There are two axes. The vertical is *relationship*, which is either *personal* and non-financial, or *professional* and therefore by definition, financially-based.

The horizontal axis, *realm*, juxtaposes the *public* and *private* worlds. It's the difference between what happens within a mostly closed, internal system, or that which happens open and mostly externally from any single organisation.

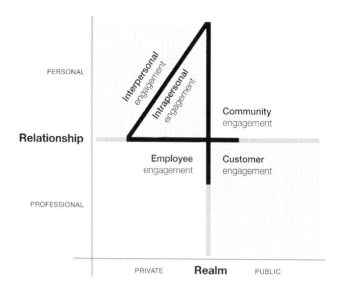

Employee engagement

The most common results from a web search on *'engagement'* (aside from engagement ring, naturally) are on the topic of employee engagement. It is the process of strengthening the relationship between employer and employee, often through the provision of a sense of a purpose that the individual can own themselves, a company culture that makes people want to be at work, and an active listening to the voice of its employees.

Professional and *private*

The frontier of employee engagement is a *professional*, financial relationship, within the closed, private realm of an organisation. Its most often a function of the HR department, although increasingly new names are being assigned to those who oversee the people part of an organisation.

On a peer level, it has much in common with inter-personal engagement (which we'll come to shortly): colleagues will likely become friends, and relationships often extend beyond professional status and become personal, and are therefore more likely to endure when a colleague transitions to another company. However for those who manage others, though they have their colleagues who are friends, they are tasked with managing personnel with whom they do not have personal connections, as is the case for department heads and executives making decisions that affect hundreds or thousands of employees.

The intention is *productivity*

What can be said of the end, the intention, of employee engagement? You'll remember that engagement is the process but not the purpose. It creates connection, which in turn fuels the intention that both parties have for the relationship. The intention for employee engagement, from the perspective of the organisation, is to improve *productivity*, usually measured by the fulfilment of a larger goal laid down in its medium-to-long-term planning. The employee will have a different view. Some will want to achieve the strategic goal, some will want a well-paid job that provides some security, and others still will want a job that they enjoy.

In response to the needs of managers to deliver these intentions, employee engagement has become an industry in its own right. Alliances, awards and conferences abound, and a large offering of tools is available to help organisations engage their employees, although sadly, many of these tools reduce employee engagement down to taking a survey and applying what is reported back. As we saw with Shape 2, the Engage-Vent, that is not engagement, but merely interaction upon which engagement can be built. It is a starting block, but it seems that all too many organisations survey their employees and then do nothing with it – classic *Engagement as Expression* level of maturity – and as such, employee morale actually decreases in response to this hypocritical ask-then-ignore form of neglect.

In startup culture, gimmick-driven workplaces complete with ping pong tables and PlayStations has become something of a cliché, in attempt to create playful work environments and inject a manufactured sense of culture. Even big bonuses, whilst appreciated by those who get them, are not a prophylactic against the woes of inconsistency in the workplace.

Far better is where organisations have invested in leadership development on an individual level, and have embraced the discipline of Internal Communications (IC) for the organisation at large. IC is akin to internal marketing and emphasises telling the narrative of an organisation, which is a vital tool for creating a sense of purpose, and reinforcing company culture. It is scattering the seeds of the company's message, recognising that within a large organisation, its employees are as diverse and competed for as their customer base is.

The ultimate expression of employee engagement is where an organisation creates a place where people can do worthwhile work. This is work that has a clear purpose and benefit to the world (which most businesses do provide, if they think about it), and also provides clear purpose and benefit to the employees, such as good pay and flexibility around hours when required. This is far more sustainable than a survey, big bonuses, or a ping pong table, which do have a place in an organisation, but only after the critical issue of worthwhile work has been addressed.

- Have you worked in an environment where gimmicks were overemphasised, and employee voice underemphasised?

- Does your company communicate why its work is worthwhile to the staff? Does it understand if the work is worthwhile to the lives of the employees?

Customer engagement

Whilst people need their jobs, people do not need to buy a certain brand or product. Accordingly, the frontier of employee engagement enjoys a certain level of safety when compared to its customer focussed counterpart.

However in the consumer world there exists at all times a range of suppliers competing for each and every buyer, and thus the imperative for a brand to engage new and existing customers is felt all the more. They must rise above the noise to attract the new customers, and stay in front of mind to retain the existing ones. This is being addressed by the frontier of *customer* engagement.

Professional and *public*

Customer engagement is *professional*, because it's based on an offering being sold, but this takes place in an open, public realm; the marketplace, as it were.

This frontier has different names, all meaning largely the same thing, determined by who precisely is doing the engaging. *Consumer* or *customer engagement* is considered to be outbound, where the brand engages the buyer. *Brand engagement*, on the other hand, is seen as inbound, where the buyer takes the initiative to engage with the brand. To add further complexity to the different terms, the word *engagement* in a digital marketing context will refer to interaction surrounding a digital asset, such as website traffic, email open rates, video views, and social media activity, sometimes contrasted to *reach*, which is how many have only seen an update, as opposed to clicked or commented on it.

One common error within this frontier is to think of B2C and B2B customers as different forms of engagement. In fact, it is the B2B context in which engagement becomes all the more important because emotion is felt more strongly towards B2B brands than their B2C cousins. There are then further, unintuitive subsets of this frontier, most commonly *partner, supplier* and *shareholder engagement*. The relationship with these is financial and professional, though they do not operate within the closed doors of the organisation, because they exist outside of it, and thus are not employee engagement, but appear here in the customer frontier. Like consumers who do not need to buy our products, suppliers and partners likewise do not *have* to work with us, and shareholders do not *need* to own their small part of the organisation. Thus matters of negotiation, finding mutually beneficial arrangements, and working to secure some sense of loyalty to one another are paramount; almost identical to the imperatives of plain customer engagement.

The intention is *profitability*

The intention of customer engagement is ostensibly increased profitability, again linked to a goal laid down in the company's strategic plan. The benefit of a customer engagement strategy is that the profitability will be incremental, sustainable, long term growth. And what of the customer's intentions? It too is *profitability*: within a balance of benefit and cost, they wish the net transaction to be profitable to them by the product itself satiating a need – another form of profitability.

For some, customer engagement is seen as synonymous with rewards and incentives, however this is confusing tactics with strategy. A reward card or incentive programme may indeed be part of a customer engagement strategy, but these are merely tools that reinforce the infinitely bigger issues of meaning, ability, transformation, and the emotional benefits that these infer.

In particular, the most successful customer engagement, as we saw in the 3-E Model, is where multiple forms of enablement are provided to the customer. This means that attention is given to the customer in order to truly understand their needs, listen to their voice, and deliver what will enable them.

And you?

- What is the profit the *customer* gets from being highly engaged with your products and company? Is that result also profitable to the company?
- How have you felt as a customer when given incentives in place of attention?

Community engagement

What about engagement that goes beyond the *professional*, and the transaction and exchange of finance as the basis for the relationship? What about where people are connected to each other because of a non-financial factor, such as location, interest or belief?

This is community engagement. As we'll see, it is a blurrier definition than customer and employee engagement, although it also boasts a large number of alternate names, some of which are highly technical and precise. Let's begin by examining it within our two axis.

Personal and *public*

Community engagement is normally *personal* and non-financially based, as we've just said, and it's generally *public*. This is not to say there are not private communities, but most communities do not exist within a formal, financial entity that requires a contract to join. As it's often said, most communities are for anyone, although they may not be for everyone.

Of all the alternate names that can be given to a frontier of engagement, this one has the most. Consider these terms, which mean varying things depending on who is using them:

- *Public engagement*, the formal name for when universities encourage their research to be engaged with by non-academics.
- *Civic engagement*, which describes the public interacting with politics and government.
- *Community engagement*, which can describe the reverse of civic engagement, where politicians or councils engage with local communities.
- *Public participation*, which tends to describe civic and community engagement within a local or regional context with or from a public institution, such as a library, museum, council or other service.
- *Community engagement* (again!), this time as a technical term used by planners to engage with local communities before they do any building or development there.
- *Community engagement* (yet again!), used to describe engagement within an online community, such as a forum or

social media page (and having a certain financial, *customer engagement* bent to it).

- *Social engagement*, which is people's involvement in groups (although can be confused as a shorthand for social media engagement).
- *Stakeholder engagement*, which describes the process of engaging those who have ownership or strong links to the outcomes of a project or organisation.
- *Corporate engagement*, a lesser used term to describe partnerships pertaining to corporate social responsibility.

The above does not include the non-technical terms that fall within this frontier that give a specific title to the community being engaged, such as *parent* or *student engagement* within the context of schools and universities.

Therefore, because of the blurrier definition of *community* when compared to the more binary terms of *employee* and *customer* (which one either is or is not), this frontier can be blended into the other frontiers. Examples include communities of players of a particular game, communities of fans of a certain TV series, or users of a specific software package. These are communities formed around a product. Sports fans act like communities but are also ostensibly customers, and professional communities (sometimes called *communities of purpose*) are made up of people who share common jobs and partake of these groups to better their professional abilities, such as with professional associations.

So what is the dividing line between what is community engagement, and what is customer or employee engagement? The answer lies in remembering that the frontier of community engagement is the *personal* rather than *professional* reflection of these two other frontiers. Therefore, whilst the professional element is an important part of any of the communities we've listed above, the community is bigger than that relationship, and can survive without it if need be. A supporter's club of a sports team will have attending games as a core activity, but the club is certainly more than *just* that, and the members would be the first to say so.

The intention is *purpose*

The intention for community engagement is the fulfilment of *purpose*. All communities will have an aim or a goal, very often in the form of some potential being realised (generally a socio-economic goal in a local community), and accordingly the intention is the achievement of that.

We will not be surprised to find that the member of the community again wants the same thing as the organisation, which in this case is the fulfilment of their own purpose of being in that community, the particulars of which will differ from person to person, but the overarching theme being that the benefits matter to their life, and will match the 3-E Maturity Model in their progression of maturity.

A common illusion, particularly in the public sector and those organisations engaging with a local community, is that community engagement is a checkbox exercise that a direct or blanket mailing will tick. This is a far cry from talk of purpose.

I have heard many a frustrated project manager relate how they've "engaged the community" but didn't have any response to the letters they posted through the doors. Thinking back to the 3-E Model, we can clearly see this as Engagement as Expression, with folded arms!

Employers and marketers can get away with lower engagement of their employees and customers to a certain extent, yet still call their activity engagement. This is not the case for communities. A community that is not at the level of Engagement as Experience – which is to say it is a community that has gathered together – has not been and is not engaged. A community must gather to be a community, even if that gathering means they all live in the same zip or postal code.

And you?

- What is the shared purpose for your community and its members? Think back to the Intention level of the Engage-Vent.
- How effective have you found broadcast mailings compared to more social tactics like gathering and events?

Interpersonal engagement

The three frontiers that we've looked at are those frontiers that are most formalised, to the point of becoming industries in and of themselves. But all of them are extensions of one common basis: *interpersonal engagement*. Marked by the diagonal corner of the number 4, this is the engagement frontier that all others are built on. In fact, customer, employee or community engagement are merely interpersonal engagement at scale. It's often said, for instance, that employees don't leave companies they leave managers. Well, this is why.

Personal and private

Any relationship that is actual rather than theoretical is interpersonal, such as colleagues versus the masses of employees within a company that don't know each other. It is *personal*, owned by an individual at a non-financial level, and it's *private*, confined to the relationship within which it happens.

At its most essential level, interpersonal engagement is the place of friendship and family, but perhaps more relevant for readers of this book, it is the place of peers, partners and audiences. For instance when I am coaching someone to deliver a speech or get a particular client engaged, I consider this to fall under interpersonal engagement. This indeed is a bit blurry. An audience may have paid to listen to your speech, and a client would pay you for your offering. But what distinguishes these relationships at that particular point in time is just how close quarters they are: they are often face-to-face, at a specific time, with a high degree of focus on one another. They are so close, in fact, that one cannot help but have an equally personal and professional bond with them. Likewise, two colleagues who cannot get on is not an issue of employee engagement. This is an issue of interpersonal engagement as much as two children who keep on clashing at school, or two family members who cannot get on.

Interpersonal engagement is not yet formally an industry by name, nor is it likely to be so, as it is certainly well represented in the personal development shelf of any book shop. Dale Carnegie's quintessential personal development title, *How to Win Friends and Influence People* is an interpersonal engagement if ever there was one, as are the thousands of business books released every year since, right up to this day, that follow in its vein.

The intention is *propitiousness*

The intention of both parties within interpersonal engagement is for the relationship to be *propitious*, for whether it is a friendship, family member or colleague at work, what we ultimately want is favourable conditions on both sides; to give to and get from the relationship, in accordance with the maxim that engagement is to make the most of a relationship.

Sadly many have come to approach their relationships with tactics such as feedback sandwiches, looking to templates that can be applied to improve their relational approach. This is not to put down the roll of training, but interpersonal engagement, such as with family and friends, is based on genuine bonds rather than modelled behaviour.

Of all the frontiers, interpersonal engagement is the most like an art form: reading the person in front of you, knowing their past history, and using that to determine your approach, and navigate what you wish to bring into and out of the relationship.

<hr>

And you?

<hr>

- How have you seen others excel at creating propitious relationships? What can you learn from them about interpersonal engagement?

Intrapersonal engagement

If there were just four frontiers of engagement we'd have finished by now, but in the name of novelty, perhaps insight, and hopefully memorability, there is a fascinating extra half-a-frontier still left for us to explore.

For the longest of times I was trying to find a way to marry my love of engagement of others, with my love for the engagement of the self, i.e. self understanding, spirituality and personal development. I intuitively felt they were two sides of the same coin, but it seemed like I was trying to melt two separate coins together to make that work, that is until I saw the empty space inside the diagonal line on the number 4.

If interpersonal engagement is the basis of the three other frontiers, then this final frontier is certainly the basis for all of them, and its name is *intrapersonal engagement*.

Personal and *private*

Beyond the personal and private nature of interpersonal engagement, this frontier of intrapersonal engagement is *deeply personal* and *private*. It is our inner world: the most personal, private and intimate place we have, where we have relationship with ourselves and ourselves alone.

This relationship with ourselves is inexorably and irrevocably linked to how we relate to others. Low self esteem will make us think too lowly of ourselves; too high a sense of self esteem will make us think lowly of others. Additionally, the extent to which we have mined our own skills and abilities – are making the most of ourselves – the more value we can in turn pass onto others.

The intention is *peacefulness*

Our intention for interpersonal engagement, and what others want for us too (for it is indeed what we all want, and want for each other) is *peacefulness*, whatever lens one views this from. Generally we tend to consider a person who is at peace to be a person who is making the most of themselves without negative emotions involved, and passes that onto others.

And you?

- What is it that you do that makes the most of yourself?
- If someone was giving your coaching, what would they likely say to you?

- Do you have a process of engaging with yourself, such as journalling, regular therapy, or coaching?

4-and-a-half at once: Enterprise Engagement

Finally for this shape, what happens when an organisation pursues engagement across all frontiers, and across everyone involved in the value chain?

The answer is *Enterprise Engagement*, and today's executive must be a master at it. Their working week will span from motivating their workforce, dazzling their customers, pleasing their partners, satisfying their shareholders, interacting with their peers, and speaking to communities; they will they endeavour to make the most of all those relationships, all the while ensuring that they are making the most of themselves and their unique skills.

By discerning the different frontiers of engagement, they have the strategic advantage of approaching each one differently, according to what the need is. They can also structure their team accordingly, often by having a lead on each of the frontiers.

And you?

- Who have you noticed within your organisation that should be engaged in decisions, but isn't because of a hierarchical or historical reason?
- What would your organisation look like if everyone in the value chain was engaged?

* * *

The 4-and-a-half Frontiers of Engagement • Reference Table

Frontier	Relationship	Realm	Goal
Employee	Professional	Private	Productivity
Customer	Professional	Public	Profitability
Community	Personal	Public	Purpose
Interpersonal	Personal	Private	Propitiousness
Intrapersonal	Personal	Private	Peacefulness

OVE4＊X&

Shape 5

The Five Spurs of Engagement

When are people motivated to engage?

We've spent most of our time up until now thinking strategically, albeit with a nod to tactics here and there. What if we were to pause that for a moment and focus solely on those tactics, and explore what the actionable motivators behind engagement are, what would we do? That's the aim of this shape. Of course, we won't be leaving our strategic understanding behind, for it greatly enriches our understanding of the tactics. But if there is to be a supremely practical, *how-to* shape, this is it.

These five spurs are what motivate engagement, or more precisely, are the conditions under which people are motivated to engage. For this framework is not a matter of *what*, but *when*.

This is an important distinction. To ask 'what must we do to motivate people to engage?' is a question that assumes that people by default do not want to engage, unless correctly motivated.

However, to ask 'when do people engage?' is concordant with my view that people are constantly in the Circle of Engagement – ready, waiting and wanting to be engaged – and when the conditions are met, the initiator and the receiver attract like a magnet. To extend the metaphor, the point then is to use the spurs to sharpen your magnet!

The Five Spurs of Engagement is the shape of an asterisk, which in most fonts will have five points, one for each spur. The five spurs are also an acronym of *Spurs*: *Shared*, *Prompt*, *Understanding*, *Response* and *Sensibility*.

The shape itself, although as asterisk, looks like the spurs from cowboy boots, certainly something that when pressed into the skin draws a reaction!

We can also see what each spur motivates, and what it obstacle it overcomes as a result:

- The shared spur overcomes ambivalence
- The prompt spur overcomes forgetfulness
- The understanding spur overcomes confusion
- The response spur overcomes inertia
- The sensibility spur overcomes apathy

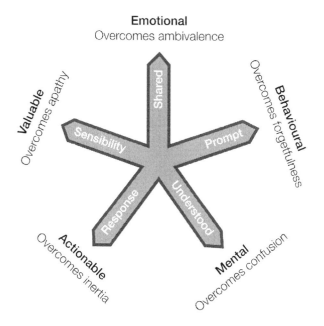

Emotional
Overcomes ambivalence

Shared

It is perhaps so obviously apparent that we might forget to actually say it, but something *engages* you because it engages *you*: your personality, history, feelings and ambitions. In other words, we like people and things that we share something in common with. We care about what we have in common, because it means to care for one's self, and one's interests and desires.

If you're a fan of a particular sports team, you always spot it when someone wears your team's logo. Or if you've recently had a baby, you'll immediately notice heavily pregnant women and empathise. Or if you've just passed your driving test, you'll notice advertisements targeted at new drivers!

It is the intrinsic *emotional* motivator

The shared spur bypasses mental filters and elicits a response based on our most emotional instincts. We are hardwired to connect through commonality because it is a mental heuristic for finding validation and safety. When we see or hear something that has shared commonality our response is nigh-subconscious and automatic, even to a physiological level: look at how someone smiles involuntarily when given good news, or freezes when given bad news.

In this way, the shared spur is like an autoresponder. If you're in a foreign country and you hear your home language and accent, your ears will *instantly* perk up like a dogs, without a moment of thought about whether you wish to engage with it or not.

In fact, based on this, a practice that I keep is to learn small pieces of many languages so that I can quickly create a bond of trust with those from other countries, wherever they may be from, because of the commonality that I have displayed, which is a sign of my empathy towards them, and a signal of safety.

It overcomes the obstacle of *ambivalence*

We are ambivalent to most things that seek to engage us, likely not even acknowledging their attempts, because we have high sophisticated filters that weed out the large volume of messaging noise that we don't share commonality with.

But when we do share something in common and automatically respond, as we've described above, as a result, even if it is only ever in the form of aspiration and unrealised desire, this obstacle of ambivalence is overcome.

Therefore, the brand at the Engagement as Expression level of maturity will only be met with ambivalence if it does not find a shared spur to connect with. It is all too common for messages from companies to be loaded with their own branding but nothing that communicates what is in common beyond that.

However, if the shared spur is motivated, it all but guarantees that the receiver will respond in some way. This is particularly important within the transition between the Scatter and Gather process, where one goes from being a receiver to a responder. When the shared spur is motivated, people automatically respond and often quickly gather because of how it affects the subconscious. It therefore follows that a company that resonates with the shared spur will very frequently move into the Engagement as Experience level of maturity.

This is what the marketing discipline of niching is about: speaking to a target market so narrowly that those you communicate with cannot help but respond to the high level of commonality that is expressed.

Finally, as we get into the Engagement as Enablement level, what is shared tends to shift from a common past or a common present to a common future, such as shared meaning, actualisation, and purpose.

And you?

- Do people see people like themselves in your messaging? Do they see language like their own? Are there experiences that they share that are emphasised?

- What is someone's subconscious reaction to your message? Have you spent time understanding what feelings your message provokes?

Prompt

All engagement would remain unrealised if there was not something to prompt it. Think of this as the cause, or the trigger. On a low level of maturity this could be an advert or email, going right up to the high level of maturity where someone has a built in habit that prompts a certain engagement ritual. But whether it's a habit, an advert, an event, or clocking in for work at 9am, all of these are prompts, or triggers, to engage.

It is the intrinsic *behavioural* motivator

The prompt works because the receiver is looking for a prompt, in line with their personal intentions. We could call it an excuse to act. Notifications on your phone, a set time for dinner, putting a meeting in the diary for 2pm next Tuesday: all of these are prompts.

Often a prompt becomes a tool of automation, stacked onto habits. Consider the various apps on our phone. At first an app itches an emotion, say curiosity or ambition. Many apps don't successfully scratch that itch and get deleted. Then, we use it because there's an interaction within which it's useful. Finally, The holy grail is when the app moves to our home screen because everyday is a prompt to use it, like when we check Instagram in the morning, finish a workout and enter our routine, or send our family photos to a shared WhatsApp group.

It overcomes the obstacle of *forgetfulness*

Many an engagement opportunity is lost not for lack of desire or due to neglect, but simply because of forgetfulness. Life gets in the way! A prompt overcomes forgetfulness by triggering our action there and then. This has become a particular fashion in internet marketing today where so-called 'squeeze pages' prompt action there and then through scarcity techniques, and follow up with automated email sequences, so that their prospect cannot forget to act! They will either act or unsubscribe!

Such processes aren't my cup of tea, but they are popular for the reason that they are highly effective at drawing out action because of how clear and consistent the prompt is.

As seen in the example of the app getting to the home screen on our phone, the prompt spur escalates from a low, more incidental cause for interaction, eventually getting to a habitual cause. In a religious community, for instance, the prompt initially is the message of that community, received by a newcomer (Engagement as Expression). However, the prompt soon changes for the new comer, who is now a regular, to be the weekly meeting time (Engagement as Experience). Finally, at the highest level of maturity, the regular has become deeply passionate, and has daily spiritual rituals which they draw energy from and even shape their day around (Engagement as Enablement).

And you?

- When are people motivated to engage with you? What locations, times, and scenarios acts as prompts?

- Can you stack prompts on top of existing habits and rituals with your customers, employees, and community members? Think about what actions they already do, and what scope there is for building on that.

Understanding

From film plots to knowing historical facts, and from sporting knowledge to knowing the answer to a riddle, we enjoy understanding and having mastery within a subject. It's why pub quizzes and Trivial Pursuit are popular, and why we get so frustrated when we ourselves or someone else don't 'get' something.

It is the intrinsic *mental* motivator

It is entirely about engaging our processing and rational faculties by making something understandable and clear. It acts like reading glasses. Glasses serve to focus what is in view, compensating for either long or short sightedness. When something is too far it doesn't tell us enough. When something is too close, it tells us too much. In both cases, it's out of focus, and we can't discern what is in front of us. Thus, we have the Goldilocks nature of the understanding spur: not too little, not too much, but just right.

The desire to understand has incredible motivational power. It's why we are drawn to lists of '10 reasons why', frameworks and models, and how-to's: they make things clear for us. When something is clear, and we comprehend it, we resonate because of the feeling of success and stature that we derive. It's that moment when something 'clicks', the penny drops, and we now grasp what it's about.

Indeed, the mind craves clarity. We are looking for it. Even when we are engaging with something mysterious, such as an intriguing film plot, or trying something new that isn't entirely clear to us yet, we understand that we are indeed engaging with a mystery or something new, and thus the intention that we are to discover the solution or master the skills is plain to us. (This is why we are frustrated by loose ends in a plot or a cliffhanger: the deal of a mystery is that all will be explained by the end! But it also explains why they are so intensely engaging: we must close the loop and we'll go and see the next film to do that!)

It overcomes the obstacle of *confusion*

Coming back to the land of stating the obvious, a major blockage to engagement is when we don't understand what we are being engaged by or what we are being asked to engage with. I've experienced my fair share of this: not on the receiving end, on the initiating end. I do a large amount of facilitating group sessions, but every once in a while I will phrase a question terribly, and as I wait in silence for the group to answer, after about 20 seconds someone will say "what do you mean by that question?" In other words, it's as clear as mud and we didn't get it!

I imagine that we've all suffered from over-complicating issues at one time or another. We will have all seen the power of when, having made it clearer by rephrasing it, our receiver gets it. That's what the understanding spur does: it ensures people have clarity, for without it, engagement will get lost in the mist of confusion.

At every level of maturity, the understanding spur ensures that a lack of clarity does not stand in the way of people engaging. It's particularly important within the Scattering process, because people cannot engage with a message unless they understand what it is. It is also vital in the Matter process, because to be enabled we must understand how to benefit from that which enables us, even if it is just on an basic level.

And you?

- Is your offering clear and understandable? Does someone get what you're about when they receive your message?
- Do people know the benefits of engaging with you?

Response

We established in the 3-E Maturity Model, that for engagement to go beyond the first level of maturity the message must be responded to. The response spur is specifically about providing a clear and simple cue for people to respond to. If someone is suffering from low engagement, it is often likely that there is not a clear cue or clear call to action to respond to.

The response spur can be confused with the prompt spur, as they respectively speak to action and behaviour. The difference is that a prompt is a behavioural trigger, where as the response is the clear action to take based on that trigger, which we'll look at next:

It is the intrinsic *actionable* motivator

If we have successful connected through the shared spur, we might have a pleasant connection, but without the response spur, it will go no further.

Response is critical if we are to progress from Engagement as *Expression* to Engagement as *Experience*. Mere expression, as part of the Scatter process, does not require a response. It is engaging because we are entertained by it, albeit it ephemerally.

To progress we must activate the Gather process, which requires receivers to become responders by responding to something. This is what the response spur provides.

Think of it as the button that is pressed to activate further engagement. It can be as literal as a button on a website or link in an email, but it's often akin to "rase your hand if…": the simple act of someone raising their hand in a lesson, answering a question, asking a store clerk for assistance, ordering from the menu, pointing to what you want, and so forth.

All of these are actions, and actions of response. They are what transitions a receiver into a responder.

It overcomes the obstacle of *inertia*

The response spur overcomes inertia. We often don't have the motivation to think about what to do next, even if only a little thought is required to figure it out, because inertia so quickly sets in. The response spur solves this by telling us what to do to respond. Put simply, if someone asks us to engage, we are more likely to do it. This is simply because life is busy, we often don't take the initiative, thus we like people to tell us what to do.

If you're getting low engagement, it might simply be because you're not asking for a response. One quick way to boost engagement therefore is to make something an *invitation* rather than just *information*, for we all know what to do with an invitation: accept or decline (or ignore, which is to decline).

Another quick way is to ask a question, for we all know what a question mark means, and a response is easy for us, especially if it is within the context of something shared.

And you?

- Do your messages have calls to action and response buttons built into them? Is it incredibly clear what someone is to do if they want to respond to your message?

- Have you asked questions on social media? If so, have they been successful at getting engagement? What other symbols can you use to encourage response?

Sensibility

People love to engage in three things: things that are spreadable (as in, it's popular within my circle), things that are shareable (as in, I can share in them), and things that are scaleable (they help me scale my life). These are the three attributes that make something valuable as an entity for engagement.

When a receiver makes the decision to engage, their sensibility – the perception and responsiveness – is based upon these three points of value which illicitly demonstrate what the receiver will get from the engagement.

It is the intrinsic *valuable* motivator

Something or someone that does not embody the attributes listed above will not be deemed of value as far as engagement goes. Without them they will deem that entity as being unable to provide meaningful engagement, or sustainable engagement, or both.

We can view this as a cost-benefit ratio. Is my benefit of engagement more than the cost of engagement that I will pay? This is not necessarily communicated mentally, as in the case of the understanding spur. It is less about listing benefits on a sheet, and more about demonstrating them through what the engagement actually does.

Now it is true that people will at times engage with entities that are not very spreadable, shareable or scaleable. This might be because the engagement is with a friend or a friend's organisation, or came via a recommendation. It might even have been that the entity appeared worthy of engagement, but turned out not to be so. In such cases, 'engager's remorse' is to be expected. This is where the transaction occurs, but none of the other, more transformational benefits of engagement ensue: there is no loyalty, no recurring engagement, no advocacy. In fact, it might have a detrimental affect, whereby the receiver becomes a detractor to the entity.

To guard against such remorse, one must manage expectations, ensure they deliver that which is at least moderately spreadable, shareable or scalable in accordance with the maturity of the engagement offering, and certainly be careful they do not over promise and under deliver.

It overcomes the obstacle of *apathy*

Correctly applied, the sensibility spur overcomes the obstacle of apathy. Where the shared spur, which is emotionally focused, overcomes ambivalence and makes something resonate through commonality, the sensibility spur ensures apathy does not set in after the initial interaction by demonstrating the value of the engagement, as verified by others.

Many a potential engagement is lost where someone is a receiver, but upon closer inspection, decides not to engage further and become a responder because there is not enough value in the engagement: apathy has set in where there was once interest.

And you?

- Does your messaging convey that others are spreading your message, and that others are sharing in your gathering moments?

- How could you use numbers and pictures to affirm the value that others find in engaging with you?

* * *

The Five Spurs of Engagement • Reference Table

Spur	Intrinsic	Overcomes
Shared	Emotional	Ambivalence
Prompt	Behavioural	Forgetfulness
Understanding	Mental	Confusion
Response	Actionable	Inertia
Sensibility	Valuable	Apathy

OVE4 ✳ **X** &

The X Marks the Spot

Which of the six stages of engagement are people at?

In the 3-E Maturity Model we looked at the journey an organisation goes through as it increases its own engagement capabilities. It will start at Engagement as Expression, where it is mostly concerned with scattering its message. It will then progress to Engagement as Experience, where it gathers and interacts with responders through a medium and in a moment. Finally, it will reach Engagement as Enablement, where it matters to cooperators because it provides means and meaning.

But what of the journey that the receiver of our engagement goes through? What is like for them to go from a receiver to responder to cooperator, and from having an ephemeral connection, to an eventful connection, to an enduring connection? How do we build this kind of long lasting connection that is based on meaning, purpose, and enablement?

The receiver, too, goes through the 3-E Maturity model, however the precise psychological stages of their journey are a bit more gradual than the broader processes of Scatter, Gather, and Matter. What we will find below is that the three processes of Scatter, Gather, Matter are each split into two stages, totalling six overall psychological stages.

Not all people will engage at the highest level. Think back again to our discussion that engagement with any entity, be it a person, brand, product, or idea is the same. In human relationships, we generally tend to have a small group of highly engaged friends and a higher volume group of acquaintances. In the same way, a product might have a small number of highly engaged cooperators compared to a larger volume of receivers and responders.

X

The X Marks the Spot is an X, with the Scatter, Gather, Matter process running horizontally through the middle of it.

From left to right are the six psychological stages of engagement, from *acknowledge*, up to *enlist*. There are two stages to each of the three Scatter, Gather, Matter processes.

The left side of the X is where the Scatter process happens. This is a place of high volume, low value, just like we'd expect considering that this process is about scattering a message, encouraging other to spread the message, and embracing the role of chance throughout all of it.

The right side of the X is, by contrast, a place of low volume, high value, also what we expect when talking about mattering through means and meaning: two high value things that in general we expect less of our people to connect with.

In the middle of the X – where X marks the spot! – we have the shared moment that we have talked so much about, which is the hallmark of the Gather process, and the very thing that its offering, Engagement as Experience, provides.

Unless the receiver of our engagement becomes a responder, and gathers around our offering, they cannot go on to become a cooperator with us and be enabled the platform that we provide. Thus, the Gather process is not just another part of engagement, but the doorway from low value to high value connection, for both the receiver and the initiator. This marks the transition from engagement being based on *reason* to being based on *relationship*.

The X Marks the Spot

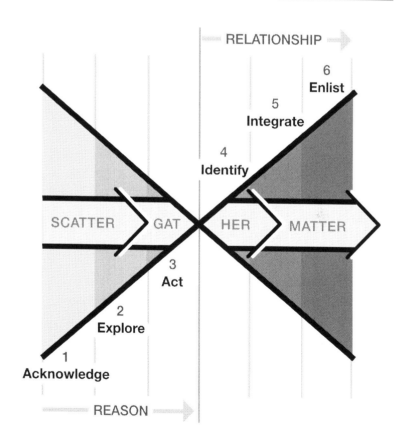

Scatter

As the first process of engagement is messaging from initiator to receiver (the first half of the stimulus-response loop), the two psychological stages within this process are about what a receiver does when they receive a message.

Stage 1: Acknowledge

We know that all engagement begins with a message. But for the receiver, all engagement begins with the simple acknowledgement that they are indeed being engaged by a message.

Messages are endlessly put out to us. Yet those that we do not acknowledge, that is, that we do not emotionally and cognitively take note of, fall to the ground and bear no fruit. These messages are the ones to which the Spurs of Engagement are not intrinsically motivated. However, if a message gets through to us, and if we acknowledge it, and if we remember it, then we have engaged with it because it has touched in particular our shared spur. This spur is what is causes a subconscious reaction to messages because there is commonality between us and it, which is the most frequent reason for us to acknowledge something.

It is what we *see and hear*

Acknowledgement happens by seeing or hearing something. It's about what comes to us, rather than what we are seeking. This is to be expected, given we are in the Scatter process, which is ostensibly about communicating the message.

It is useful to know this, because engagement cannot begin but be communicated through these senses: a customer cannot read the brand's mind, they must see or hear!

Use the *Virus* strategy

A third party endorsement is more powerful that a branded message, because it is more trusted: we expect a branded message to lack objectivity, but believe third parties to have it.

The organisational sensibility for the Scatter process is that the message can spread from person to person, which is the way to get people to acknowledge you via third party endorsement. As the old proverb goes, "Let another's lips praise you, and not your own." To achieve this, make the message compelling. Make it something remarkable, that motivates the Spurs of Engagement, and is hard *not* to talk about.

And you?

- Where do people see and hear your message? What are the channels that you use to reach people?
- How do you know your receivers have acknowledged it?
- Do people talk about your message? What do they say?

Stage 2: Explore

If our prompt spur is motivated upon receipt of the message, because an emotional need or desire is resonating, then we will go to the next step to explore more about the message. This is a fact finding mission: what is the provenance of this seed that has been scatted to us? What is it about? What is it offering us? What are the benefits and outcomes?

Explorations activities include visiting a website, doing online research, asking a friend, checking it out yourself, and so on. If a job advert is seeking to engage us, we'll explore by reading the job specification. If an advert is seeking to engage us, we'll do a bit more research online. If we're asked for a meeting, we'll check out someone's LinkedIn profile.

It is what we *unbox*

The trend for unboxing, where people document the unpacking of a product, is a perfect analogue for how we explore. Exploration is about learning by dismantling and filling in the blacks. When someone has acknowledged you, and the prompt spur is motivated, and the response spur is pointing them where to go next, they will proceed to discover what they can about you, completing the gaps in their knowledge.

If, as a result of our initial acknowledgement, and now our exploration, if all the Spurs of Engagement are intrinsically motivated, especially the understanding spur because we have successful inboxed the invitation to engage, then we'll proceed onto the next stage, which takes us into the Gather process.

Use the *Menu* strategy

To help people access you, consider making your message a menu that has a starter, main, and dessert.

Create a simple version of the message that is the starter. Then a full version, which is the main. Finally, the dessert is the bonus, the exciting extra, that can't be ignored! But whatever you do, don't throw it all at people at once.

Imagine that you are the server, guiding people through the menu, highlighting each course and options at the suitable time.

- How do people find out more about your message? For instance, how would an employee find out more about an internal project that is happening?

- Have you made it easy for people to unbox you? Do you have a playlist or menu with the options that people can browse, putting the most relevant things first?

Gather

The second process of engagement is predicated on a receiver becoming a responder (the second half of stimulus-response). Here the initiator seeks to gather those who respond to themselves, and to other responders.

The offering here is that of Engagement as Experience. It's a place of interaction, happening within a medium in a specific, shared moment. It is tactical, actionable, and participatory.

Stage 3: Action

If the response spur is motivated, because it's clear what we should do to engage next, the receiver will become a responder by taking action. Having explored the offering, we now experience it, gather to it, interact with it, and share a moment with it: we enter the store, we use the app, we pick up the tool, we buy the product, we watch the film, we go on the date, we attend the service, we watch the game, attend the interview or regularly go to work, and so forth. Additionally, we may have gathered to the other responders, in the store, on the social network, at the game, during the service, at our workplace, etc.

As you can imagine, we could easily stop at this stage, and many do. Most people take action and become users, members, employees, and customers, and stay there, failing to be engaged by further. Think of the hundreds of millions of knowledge workers who use the same software every day, but would not likely say that they are engaged by it. It is a tool of convenience, not of conviction.

It is what we *do*

The Gather process is about a receiver becoming a responder. Thus, this stage of action is about what we do. The offering at this level is Engagement as Experience, and the intensity of how engaging it is will be marked by how much we can share in it.

To begin, this action is very positive, but over time it can become automated and stagnant. To transition from reason to relationship, one must go beyond activity to identity, as we are about to see.

Use the *Put your hand up if* strategy

At school we all learnt to respond to questions by putting our hands up. That's because a question is a response mechanism: we can either answer, or ignore.

In the same way, to get people to become responders who experience you, and as a result, do the according actions, make it easy for them. Frame your messages with calls to action that ask people to 'put up their hands if', and when they do, find a way to capture who put their hand up, and take them aside to engage with just them – just like the farmer would gather a crop into a bind, rather than trying to gather everything together at once.

Imagine this is a giant button for your responders. When you see a button, what do you do? You press it. Make it that easy and straight forward.

And you?

- What are people doing day-to-day with your offering? What is the action of your customers, employees, and community members, that they perform on a regular basis?
- Out of those interactions, which are the most experiential?

Stage 4: Identify

Moving from action to identity is how a responder moves from being on the left-hand side of the X shape to the right-hand side. By transitioning from user, member, employee or customer to an owner, such a person derives identity from the entity with which they are engaged.

These are people who have gone from engagement based on reason to engagement based on reason.

To progress to this stage, the shared and understanding spurs need to be intrinsically motivated. Within the Gather process, the shared spur means that the responder has a sense of belonging, as we've said above, combined with the understanding spur which takes the form of a narrative understanding. This means they see themselves as on a journey with the organisation.

A common and significant marker is when someone goes from calling themselves a "user of X" to an "X-er", such as one who transitions from being *someone who climbs* to a *climber*, or *someone who tweets* to a *tweeter*. When someone becomes a regular at a café or bar, and adopts their 'usual' drink, they identify with that establishment, and their individual quirks become part of that identity, such as preferring rhubarb and *mustard* over rhubarb and *custard*! Shows like Friends or Cheers point to this yearning that we have to belong and derive identity from a place that we and others gather around, a place 'where everybody knows your name'.

And that is the crucial part of this transition: gathering not just to the initiator, but to the *others*, the other responders. It is the social dynamics of these peer relationships that create the strongest of identities, for an identity means to be part of a larger whole, and each other person that is interacted with grows the sense of the whole for our responder. The more frequency we have with other responders, all the while gathering around the initiator, the greater the sense of identity we will form.

It is what we *mirror*

We form identity by first mirroring it from others. Again, this is why gathering to others, and not just to the entity, is so important. There must be visible behaviour and markers for people to see and then repeat; what to wear, what to say, how to use the product, how to hold oneself.

For many entities, mirroring is performed in a powerful way through initiation rites. Famously, in college fraternities and sororities, this takes the form of hazing and extreme rites of passage. In religion, this is marked by baptism, specific clothing, or another demonstration of faith. In some social circles, it is marked by badges or other attire signals. For some customers, it's wearing logos in prominent places. All of these actives say "I am doing what the others do: and I'm one of them."

Use the *Showcase* strategy

One of my earliest projects was running a monthly youth concert that was by young people for young people. At first attendance was very low. But then I accidentally came upon a growth technique: if I invited a band to play that had a following, their following would come along to see them perform.

So I held a battle of the bands, inviting five popular local bands to play against each other. Each brought their fans, and with that audience combined, I created my own new audience. It was rent-a-crowd for free.

This is showcase strategy. It's based on the idea that the teacher gets all the parents to come to the school play by putting all the kids in the show. When someone has skin in the game, they have greater ownership, and want others to see them in it.

To create a strong sense of identity, give people a role in the Gathering experience, and watch how it increases their own ownership, and how they bring their friends and family to watch them perform.

And you?

- How do your people gather to each other? Can they see who else is engaged with you at this level?

- What are the behaviours that people mirror at this stage? What do people do when they are "one of you"?

Matter

The third process of engagement is where responders become cooperates together with the initiators. It is a far more dynamic relationship, and as we've described in Shapes 1 and 3, a place of procreation and making new things through the platform that is made by both parties.

The offering within this process is Engagement as Enablement, so according the two stages will look at how they integrate the means and meaning it provides into their life.

Stage 5: Integrate

If the prompt and response spurs are intrinsically motivated at this point, then the responder will be experiencing regular prompts for engaging with the initiator, and have a clear response pathway for doing so. Combined, this means the responder will become a cooperator who begins integrating an enabling the platform into their life.

The prompts will have moved from emotional, to involving, and now to everyday, and will be linked to key daily rituals and habits.

The response will no longer be about what the responder should do to respond to the initiator, rather it will be about what the cooperator says the platform 'lets me' do. Gathering is about action towards and with the initiator, but in the Matter process, action is from the cooperators, and from the platform out into their lives. After all, it's about enablement.

Integrating a platform into our life also results in a certain level of exclusivity. By integrating one platform, we are saying no to the others that are available.

It is what we *immerse in*

The reason why this stage is marked by exclusivity is because we engage in such an immersive way at this point. We regularly see this with brand love. Having embraced their iPhone, a customer makes their way to owning an iPad, and finally their MacBook. Having committed to an employer and the company's mission, the employee winds down some of their other professional pursuits to go big on this career commitment. And having become a initiated member of this community, the member lets their other community interests fade away, like the person who joins a new professional association, and now stops using their old one in their email signature, even though their membership is still paid up for four more months.

Use the *Elbow* strategy

There's a popular phrase which is "to be at the elbow of the deal". The idea is that you might not be the hand that experiences the direct benefit of the deal, but you are the elbow that played a role in enabling it to happen.

And of course, given we're at the level of Engagement as Enablement, it is the elbow that enables the hand to do pretty much anything, for without it, the hand would have far greater restriction on its movement.

When helping people integrate, find out how you can be at the elbow of the benefit they are deriving. This is precisely what platform is about. Think about any hardware of software in your life, or a powerful idea that you use everyday, or a tool that you use at work. These are all elbows that enable the deal.

And you?

- What does exclusivity look like for your customers, employees, and communities? What competitors do they end their relationship with because they are highly engaged with you?

- Does your platform help people integrate your offering into their lives? What examples do you have from your own personal life of tools that helped you integrate them into your life?

- How does the integration stage compare to the action stage? What is the difference in activity between an "average user" and "super user"?

Stage 6: Enlist

The highest psychological stage is where the cooperator begins a formal relationship with the initiator, working alongside them to fulfil the mission that the person, product, brand or idea has.

If we think back to Shape 2, the Engage-Vent, what we are describing here is a relationship where the top of the vent, the intention of the initiator and the cooperator are aligned.

This stage can only be reached when the organisation provides both means and meaning. Someone can be engaged at the integration stage on means alone, but to enlist in helping an organisation's mission requires one to align with matters of purpose, vision, and meaning.

Needless to say, these are the customers, employees, and community members that are in the Matter process and help create new loops of the Scatter process. To return to our farming analogy, they have eaten the meal, and are now planting new seeds alongside the farmer.

It is what we *teach*

At the integration stage we immerse ourselves by jumping in the deep end. At the enlist stage, we are the instructor on the side of the pool, teaching others what to do.

There are numerous ways for organisations to adopt this strategy themselves. Very often, if a highly engaged individual has not enlisted, it's not because they do not want to, it is because there has not been a clear enough opportunity for them to.

For further engagement, and the new loop of Scatter, Gather, Matter, these people are not just spreaders of the message: they become the message. They are seeds in and of themselves.

Use the *Mission* strategy

Everyone loves a mission, whether it's just to go to the convenience store to stock up on supplies for a fun evening with friends, or doing something utterly new that has social impact.

Your customers, employees, and community members often feel the same about your organisation: they'd love a chance to go on a mission with you, for both the impact on others, and the experience they'd get themselves. Generally a company can give an individual access to things they might not have access to regularly, such as travel, tools, people connections, and the like, and when they do, that creates a very high level of engagement, and a strong, and appreciative, connection.

I find my clients are continually surprised and delighted by how keen their people are to become a part of what they are doing. But I'm not: because I know people love a mission!

And you?

- Who is on board with your mission?
- What parts of your organisation could you open up for people to experience and be a part of in some way?
- What is the meaning that people receive from you, and could become something they help others share?

* * *

The X Marks the Spot • Reference Table

Stage	Relating Style	Action	Strategy
Acknowledge	See and Hear	Contact	Virus
Explore	Unbox	Consume	Menu
Act	Test	Connect	Raise your hand if
Identify	Mirror	Commit	Showcase
Integrate	Immerse	Conjoin	Elbow
Enlist	Teach	Cooperate	Mission

OVE4✳X&

&

The Ampersand Model

Where should we begin to engage?

Here we are! After six shapes worth of engagement, we've come to the finale. Having looked at engagement through philosophical, strategic, professional, and tactical lenses, what remains? The question we must answer, and which certainly weighs upon me if this book is to truly be of use and not just bemusement, is 'where do we begin?'

This is the operational lens.

And out of all of the shapes, this one means the most to me. I'll best express this by walking you briefly through the formation of the symbol itself, which will reveal to you why it is so significant to our conversation.

Visually, the ampersand began its life as the Latin *et*, for the word *and*. Over time the *e* and *t* merged to create the *&* glyph that we all know and love. So it means 'and' – to combine two things – but also visually is a combination of two letters. However, that's not the end of the story. In the British grammar schools of the late

1800s, the alphabet was not 26 but actually 27 letters long: the last being &, the ampersand. At the time, the symbol had no name, so when reciting the alphabet, they would say "X, Y, Z, and *per se* and." Again, over time, that phrase phonetically slurred from *and per se and* to *ampersand*.

Thus the ampersand's meaning is 'together', its visual appearance is a result of two things coming together, and its phonetic rendering is the result of words coming together! Truly, a symbol that means in every way, togetherness.

So it is only fitting, when talking about engagement, which is to make the most of a relationship, that the ampersand makes an appearance, most pertinently perhaps at this point, for it is the shape that brings all the other shapes together, and demonstrates how your organisation can likewise engage and bring all of its people together.

&

The Ampersand Model, obviously in the shape of an ampersand, has four steps.

Following the direction of the arrows, we start at the bottom right-hand corner. This is labelled as Matter, for it begins with what you *already do* that matters to your customers, employees and/or community members. Just like the iterating version of the Circle of Engagement (Shape 1), this is the Matter process that a new loop can be built on.

We then proceed to the top of the shape. This is labelled as Scatter, and is the start of a new Scatter, Gather, Matter loop.

The third step is from the top-right, and folds back over the Scatter line. This is the Gather process. The folding back is significant: for people respond *to* the message, just like this line folds back on the one before it.

Finally, the fourth step is the Matter process within our new loop. It goes to the bottom left, and then folds over our original Matter step, upgrading it if you will, and then going off to the far right and beyond.

The Ampersand Model

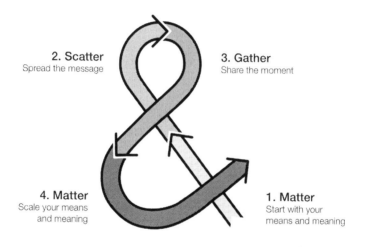

2. Scatter
Spread the message

3. Gather
Share the moment

4. Matter
Scale your means
and meaning

1. Matter
Start with your
means and meaning

Step 1: Matter

We said back in Shape 1 that all engagement begins with a message. But all messages come from a context, and as both individuals and as organisations, that is the context of what we already have, do, and are. Indeed, the Iterating Cycle of Engagement showed us that any scattering will come from what mattered before.

So as an organisation, what do you do that matters? What are the activities that you are already doing? What is the existing engagement around your offering? What is the asset that you can begin with?

The answer to these questions will be found through the time-honoured tradition of an audit:

Audit with the *Engage-Vent*

In Shape 2 we looked at the five units of relationship, from the smallest interaction, through to the overarching intention.

This will be where we begin.

Using the Enage-Vent, start from the top and plot the what, why, when, how, where, and who of your organisation against each unit.

Like most audits and other strategic exercises, this will require you to grasp with some uncomfortable realities and bring you face-to-face with some organisational contradictions. I've often found when working with clients that their stated *intention* cannot be achieved through their *interactions*. Often what entails is a more sober re-rendering of their departmental mission, which is actually a win: it brings clarity to mission and vision statements that have perhaps become too philosophical for practical use.

For this is the benefit of the Engage-Vent. By breaking down relationship into these units, down to very practical interactions such as click, type, tap, watch, listen, speak, we are forced to grapple with what really is happening when we talk about grander ideas of engagement and connection. Appreciating this will ground our efforts and makes them more impacting.

One key question to ask yourself in the audit also relates to the top psychological level of engagement as per Shape 6: who is already enlisted, and therefore highly engaged? They are the people who are already likely scattering content that others will consume. They are one of your main assets for moving forward with any further engagement.

And you?

- What is your organisation's intention for engagement? What is the intention of the people you're engaging?

- Think about a good friend of yours and describe what the connection is that you share with them. In the same vein, what is the connection that your customers, employees and community members share with your organisation?

- How do people engage with you and become connected? What is the mechanism, such as a community forum, coming to their job, working on a campaign, using your product, having regular meetings? Where do Scatter, Gather, Matter happen? Also, who are the people that are enlisted with you already, that are also a process of engagement for others?

- What ways can people participate in the engagement above? For instance if it's an online forum, can they respond to topics and create new topics?

- Finally what are the interactions? Think as practically as you can: click, type, watch, tap, hear, see, etc.

Step 2: Scatter

We're already discussed in Shapes 1 and 3 the process to begin engagement with someone is to scatter your message, and that's precisely what you should do here.

But we can go better than just scattering the first thing that comes into our head. Let's optimise the seed of our message, in light of the audit that we've just conducted.

Apply the *Spurs of Engagement*

This is Shape 5, where we noted that engagement is less about adding things to extrinsically motivate people, and more about removing obstacles that prevent people from being motivated.

Because we've audited our organisation from intention down to interaction, we can ensure that these spurs touch upon those different units. In short, is our engagement journey being mirrored through our message? It seems obvious, yet it can so easily be missed out. A key engagement process can be missing from a web page altogether, an activity that is critical to someone becoming a responder having merely a text link rather than button, an important detail to impart understanding being poorly written in a letter, and the organisation's intention being poorly understood by the marketing team, let along the customers!

Seldom does engagement require a genius strategic brainwave. Rather, it requires the basics to be executed well, and communicated clearly. As a consultant and advisor I too can easily lose sight of this, and get lost in advanced theory, rather than focussing on doing those basics well, with consistency.

Therefore when you read the questions below, don't dismiss them: you might find upon your audit and closer inspection that something's that should be obvious are not so!

And you?

- Remember the shared spur. How does our message show and say things that are shared and in common with our target audience? Think about how this communicates the state of connection from the Engage-Vent.

- Will the receiver understand your message? Is it obvious looking at your message what it's about? What is the process of engagement? Are the benefits and the reasons to engage clear and concise?

- How can the receiver respond to your message with ease and simplicity? Is it obvious how they respond? Have you removed any inertia to getting them to metaphorically 'click the button' and become a responder? Is there a clear way to interact?

- Why would a receiver see your message as valuable? Have you touched their spur of sensibility, and shown how your offering is spreadable, shareable, and scaleable? How does this relate to your organisation's intention?

Step 3: Gather

As we saw in Shape 6, the Gather process is the gateway for anyone to go from an ephemeral connection to an enduring connection. It requires a receiver to respond, to begin acting, and critically, to crossover from reason-based engagement to relationship-based engagement by going to the identify stage within the six stages of the X Marks the Spot model.

Where an organisation wishes to achieve higher engagement, but has a lack of response, it cannot proceed to a higher level of maturity. Anyone who has had a poor response to an idea or innovation can identify with this. Emails are sent, press releases put out, advertising paid for, requests made, yet there is little to no response. This is an infuriating level to be at when one wishes for increased engagement. We can think of the teaches who ask why their students don't respond, church ministers who rue the lack of response from their congregations, event managers left with empty rooms, and so on. The problem is as old as time: "you're talking, but no one is listening".

Yet people *are* listening. What they are not doing is responding. Engagement as Expression is a maturity level that simply does not transition receivers into responders. They likely forget the message shortly after hearing it, much like one forgetting the plot of a mediocre film shortly after watching it.

Sadly, this because Gather is the largely forgotten process of engagement. In a world of convenience and mass automation, and one that through digital technology has become quite asynchronous and less face-to-face, the art of experience design and of gathering people in a meaningful way is a rare and precious one indeed. As a former conference producer I know all too well that it's one thing to run an event, it's an entirely different thing to host an engaging, experiential event.

What is lacking most of all is gathering responders together to each other. Yet ironically, this is the most powerful tactic of them all. We saw in the Gather process in Shape 6 that in order to enter the psychological stage of identity, a responder must have others that they identify with as being a member of that social group. This is immensely difficult where responders are not gathered to each other, as the social group is either largely invisible or doesn't exist!

The farmer from Shape 1 had a particular tactic for gathering the harvest: the crop was put into binds. Binds are a way of chunking and breaking down responders into smaller, more intimate groups within the whole, that now, because of the size, are able to bond more intimately. One can think of this as mini communities within a macro community, as cohorts within a segment, or mastermind groups within a body.

Action **the** *X Marks the Spot*

Look again at the Ampersand Model, and you'll notice that an X shape is formed when the Gather line crosses over the Scatter line. That's one of the main reasons why I picked this shape, because when a receiver responds to a message they have acted but will come to the crossover, and if they do not crossover, will end up staying in a Scatter-Gather loop, bur never breakthrough into the Matter process and create an enduring connection with the entity.

The questions below will guide you to 'action the X', and help people crossover into the realm of Engagement as Enablement.

And you?

- First off, is it clear how people respond to your message? What is the interaction? What are the signals that they have responded to? Can they miss it?

- When people have become responders, they enter the act stage. What actions are they carrying out? Remember the person who uses software but doesn't identify with it, or think of someone who visits a coffee shop occasionally, but doesn't consider themselves to be a regular: what are people doing that they don't really derive identity from?

- Contrast this with someone who does identify with your organisation on a personal level. What actions are different? How is their language different? Is there an -er phrase that describes them as someone who identifies with you, such as regular, member, climber or tweeter?

- How can you gather people in the act stage around people in the identify stage, so that they can simulate what it would be like to be one of them and belong in that social group?

- What ways do you profile your identifiers in your messaging? What visuals and language do you use?

Step 4: Matter

In Shape 3 we looked at how the highest level of engagement is Engagement as Enablement, where an organisation offers means and meanings to its customers, employees and communities. Because the offering matters to those engaged with it – who we call *cooperators* – they have an enduring connection.

We also saw in Shape 6 that within this highest psychological stage is where someone formally enlists in the mission of the organisation. This is more than advocacy, which is often about cheering peers on. This is about getting out of the pool and becoming an formal instructor to others.

Because we've gone on a new Scatter, Gather, Matter cycle through this ampersand shape, we have unlocked new value through co-creation, and now the opportunity for procreation. Thus, what we can do to matter now will build on what we did to matter before, either as an addition, innovation, evolution, or maybe even revolution.

The last stage in the Ampersand Model is therefore simply about embracing what you can do to enable people.

Advance up the *3-E Maturity Model*

If you are at this stage, it means you are offering Engagement as Experience. You are more than simply expressing and messaging about your organisation, people are onboard with it in an interactive manner, but they are waiting to go further still.

To advance, transition *responders* into *cooperators* by emphasising *implementation* in addition to *interaction*.

Don't stop at your experiences: provide means and meaning for people to integrate the experience into their life. This entails capturing the co-created assets from when people gathered, and providing them as a useable suite of tools for the ongoing enablement of those assets, such as the sense of identity, desired behaviours, and practical activities. The key word here is practical. Mattering is the most practical process of the three: Scatter is a message and Gather is a moment, both of which come and go. But to Matter means to provide something people will use. Impractical means are not enabling means. They will not garner this highest level of engagement.

And you?

- What could you do that enables people? What do you already do that you could scale to be a platform? This could be an idea, a tool, a network, an email list, a community, practical support for people, etc.

- How can you help people implement the things that you've helped them discover or experience? Think about what they really come to you for, not just what you charge for or offer. What is the result that they are really looking to get?

- What problems do your customers, employees, and/or communities face? Or what opportunities do they have, that they are unable to fully realise? Can you provide a solution that helps people overcome this problem, or realise this opportunity, or both?

- Is there a sense of meaning that people get from being connected to you? Can you own that, and lead that?

The Next Loop

Life is engagement. And engagement, like life, is moving. It isn't that engagement *has* to move, *it just does*, and those who do not move with it run the risk of slowly drying up.

Just like those at the second level of maturity who must keep improving their experience, so too Engagement as Enablement must be updated with new innovations, else what was once enabling becomes common place. One only need to look at smart phone trends to see how what is an innovation one year is standard within two. The onus is on the initiator to keep lifting the restrictions on what its users are enabled to do, lest it is left behind like BETA Max.

There is also the very real threat for organisations at this maturity level if they become over focussed on enablement, and do not encourage the cooperators to spread the message. If this happens, they will cease to function at the Engagement as Enablement level, and begin to implode. When communities become like this, they go from being outward focussed to insular, at first out of an honest focus on providing value, but in the end, possessing an apathy and even antipathy towards broadening their engagement with others.

Sadly I have run communities myself that have suffered both these fates: one folded inward through insulation, and the other petered out through a lack of innovation.

The solution lies in the next loop.

And to do this, we must talk about the procreation within the Matter process, which is the ultimate expression of the togetherness that the ampersand symbol represents.

Life itself teaches us that survival is dependent on procreation. But there is a tradeoff: procreation is not duplication. It carries with it substantial investment, and uncertainty, because each procreated being is unique. The variances might not appear much when looking broadly at a species, but anyone in a family knows that while family members may bear the same surname, they can be wildly different people, and it takes investment to make those differences work for you rather than against you.

But it is this diversity that is the future of any engagement. Each pro-creation of something new through a platform will be different, and we will love both what we have created, and the means by which we created it. Immature organisations will seek to close down diversity, yet it is openness to diversity that creates the strongest ownership, because we own what we create, and the greatest act of enablement is to enable one to create their own. These are the things we celebrate and cherish the most, and remain loyal to. For instance, think of those books with concepts that changed the way you think for the better. Those ideas have gone beyond what was in the book: you have customised it to yourself, translated the ideas into your own language, and own them as someone who has not just heard them but given birth to them. Do you recommend those books with ambivalence, or with enthusiastic wholeheartedness? It's of course the latter. These are the books you buy for your team, family and friends. They are the books you share on social media, coming from the author whose new books you preorder and leave 5-star reviews for. That's the same author whose book readings you hope to be at, who you watch if they appear on a chat show, who you follow on Twitter and retweet. And why not? Their ideas have enabled your life and it is your joy to respond in kind, because you want more people to be enabled in the same way!

This is why the final arrow in the Ampersand Model points to an open space; the space for procreation.

And you?

- What will your customers, employees, and communities procreate? What will you make together with them through that procreation? (For their success is your success!)

- Are you prepared to embrace the diversity of procreation that is the peak of engagement? Are you prepared to enlist people in your organisation as per Shape 6, but let them be *them*?

- Will you practice servant leadership as you and your cooperators go beyond and into the future?

* * *

The Ampersand Model • Reference Table

Step	Action	Model
Matter	Audit	Engage-Vent
Scatter	Apply	Five Spurs of Engagement
Gather	Action	X Marks the Spot
Matter	Advance	3-E Maturity Model

OVE4✱X&

Epilogue

This to be true, I do engage my life.
— *Shakespeare*

"If all of this is true, then what do you do right now?"

As a former church pastor, I've said that phrase many a time to the people gathered at a service. No longer a minister, that's something I've not done for quite sometime now, but that question, that call to action, is one I've seen over and over again. It's a very engaging question.

In fact, it's not just an engaging question: it's an engaging technique. It's the response spur: the clear and obvious button for you to push, that transitions you from being a receiver to being a responder. For being true to my own work, I want to create an opportunity for you to respond, and eventually become a cooperator with the idea of engagement. So here's your button.

What should you do next?

What follows are a list of recommendations and next steps for putting engagement into practice:

1. Do an engagement audit – even if you do it in an hour

I've found this to be a very valuable exercise with my own clients, and one that is particularly eye opening.

I thoroughly believe that engagement is a skill that we use in conversation, in email, in writing – in everything! – but all too often we use it without intention. We engage for the sake of engaging, which I grant you is a beautiful thing, but it can miss out on making the most of the relationship.

Engagement is at its best when we know what our own intention is, and what our receiver's intention is, and then working together to achieve both.

Even if you take an hour to do this, and make it a surface one, it will yield huge benefits. Use Shapes 2 and 7, the Engage-Vent and the Ampersand Model, to help you.

2. Hold a customer / employee / community gathering

McKinsey called this a "no regrets" move, believing that time spent listening and talking with a small group of your customers, employers, or community members is always time well spent. I thoroughly agree.

The more technologically driven we become, the more face-to-face becomes a premium. Hire a relaxing, inspiring venue for a day – preferably in the countryside – and listen, share, enquire, walk, talk and dine. You won't believe how much you'll learn, how inspired everyone gets, and how highly engaged those who you invited will become as a result.

If you can't get physically in the same place, have a live video chat with people.

And make sure you don't just do it and then forget to follow up. Make it the beginning of a dialogue and journey of enablement. I once heard about a luxury drinks brand that took a group of bloggers on a European tour. Afterward, once the bloggers had posted their content, the brand never reached out to the bloggers again. What a waste.

3. Begin experimenting

There's not much more to say than that: begin experimenting! And do not fear what may go wrong: on the whole as humans, we like to be engaged, even if it is done less than exceptionally.

4. Become a member of the Enterprise Engagement Alliance

At the time of writing, the International Center of Enterprise Engagement has just been setup with the University of Texas Medical Branch, in preparation of the introduction of the new ISO 10018 standard for engagement.

Members of the Enterprise Engagement Alliance can undergo certification at Certified, Advanced and Master levels, much of which is done through an online curriculum, and provides mechanisms for ongoing development and support in this exciting business discipline.

Having acknowledged my recommendation, go and explore at TheEEA.org, and then act by joining!

* * *

It's been said that humans are meaning-makers. Thus I hope that these shapes take on meaning for you and your engagement efforts, and that when you see them on your keyboard, or around you every day, you'll remember them, maybe smile when you do, and will be able to quickly put them into practice, and make the most of your relationships.

Extend your book:
Download the Shape of Engagement resources

To help you get the most value from this book, all the models are available as a free download online. The package includes:

- The frameworks in a slide deck for presentations
- An executive summary of the book for your team
- A list of key engagement statistics and sources
- High-resolution colour images of the shapes
- Diagnostic forms to audit your engagement
- Expanded editions of the frameworks

Download for free at shapeofengagementbook.com

If you have enjoyed this book, please leave a review at Amazon.

Appendix

Scatter, Gather, Matter Comparison Table

	Scatter	**Gather**	**Matter**
What it is	Message	Moment	Means
Capability	Communication	Experience	Platform
Initiator and	Receiver	Responder	Cooperator
Tool	Seed	Bail	Meal
Participation	Button	Dot	Container
Response	Binary	Series	Fill
Energy	Push	Pull	Pulley
Direction	Out	In	Up
Says	Engage me	I'll engage you	Let's engage them
Creation	Recreation	Co-creation	Procreation
Sensibility	Spreadability	Shareability	Scaleability
Shared	Interest	Interaction	Intention
Agrarian	Sow	Reap	Feed
Greek	Logos	Pathos	Ethos
Robert's Rules	Motion	Seconded	Carried

About the Author

Scott Gould is an author, speaker, and management advisor to Fortune Global 500 companies and international NGOs.

He has spent 18 years working in a broad range of engagement contexts, from aviation to education, leadership development to national government, from media and entertainment to digital technology, and from event production to being a church pastor.

Formerly he founded one of the first Twitter hashtag communities, and ran a top-10 rated business conference, before leading a diverse inner city church. He now advises his clients on engagement strategy, and helps them to develop enduring connections with their customers, employees and communities.

Scott is chair of the UK chapter of the Enterprise Engagement Alliance, and a Fellow of the Royal Society of Arts.

He is also a poet, has a young family, and quite controversially, does not like cat memes.

scottgould.me

twitter.com/scottgould

facebook.com/scottgould

17379288R00092

Printed in Great Britain
by Amazon